ROBERT'S RULES OF ORDER

THE NEW ROBERT'S RULES OF ORDER

THE CLASSIC MANUAL OF
PARLIAMENTARY PROCEDURE

REVISED AND UPDATED EDITION
EDITED BY JOHN SHERMAN

BARNES & NOBLE
BOOKS
NEW YORK

This edition published by Barnes & Noble, Inc.

1993 Barnes & Noble Books

ISBN 0-8802-9972-X *pocket edition*
ISBN 0-7607-1646-3 *casebound*
ISBN 0-7607-1734-6 *paperback*

Printed and bound in the United States of America

99 00 01 02 ME 9 8 7 6 5 4
02 MC 9 8 7 6 5
03 MP 15 14 13 12 11 10

Contents

PART I. Rules of Order

Article I: How Business is Conducted in Deliberative Assemblies.

Article V: Subsidiary Motions

Article VI: Some Main and Unclassified Motions

Article VII: Debate

Article VIII: Vote

Article IX: Committees and Boards

Part II. Organization, Meetings, and Legal Rights of Assemblies

Article XII: Organization and Meetings.

Article XIII: Legal Rights of Assemblies and Trial of Their Members

Preface

Since its first publication in 1876, *Robert's Rules of Order* has been universally accepted as the standard manual of parliamentary procedure. Suited to the needs of clubs, societies, associations, and conventions, it provides all the information needed for the fair and proper conduct of meetings. *The New Robert's Rules of Order Revised* is the only modern edition that scrupulously respects the brilliantly designed form and detailed content of General Henry M. Robert's last revision of his classic manual. Published in 1915 after three years of intense labor, that edition nearly doubled the size of the 1893 edition, which was then rendered obsolete. The combined sales of all editions and reprints of the manual, now approaching 4,500,000 copies, attests to its indispensability.

The wisdom of respecting the time-tested form and content of General Robert's classic 1915 edition was apparent from the early stages of work on this modern revision, and was confirmed as every detail was closely examined in the effort to revise the text, not for "simplicity" but for concision and clarity of language and presentation. The original is thorough and complete; there is no need to add to its complexity or length. Though General Robert's prose is usually efficient and is disciplined by his genius for the structured presentation of information, this new edition is substantially and carefully condensed with no sacrifice of detail or nuance. Some redundancies have been retained, where they are clearly useful to emphasize a point, or where information that is provided in one section is repeated in another to allow the latter to stand independently.

Due to the universal adoption of *Robert's Rules of Order Revised*, parliamentary usage has remained essentially stable since the manual's publication in 1915. Language and usage, however, have changed considerably. As a result, in recent decades many students of *Rules of Order* have found the text difficult to follow. This new edition resolves this frustration. All archaic usages are rendered in a modern style. The complex syntax of the original is streamlined. The vocabulary is updated. Direct, declarative statement replaces the use of the passive voice and the polite but antiquated conditional and subjunctive tenses so common in the original. In rendering "chairman" as "the chair" and in its use of pronouns, this edition, though it does observe the grammatical protocol that orders gentlemen first, acknowledges the equal contribution of women to public life.

The object of *Rules of Order* is to assist a group to accomplish its work in the most effective manner.

Because the right of an individual to do as he or she pleases is incompatible with the interest of the group, there must be rules that to some degree restrain the individual. We enjoy the least of real liberty when there is no law and everyone acts without regard for others, and we know from experience that rules must be consistent. *Rules of Order* first appeared when parliamentary procedures were barely established and such manuals of parliamentary practice that were available were conflicting. It has since become the standard work in its field, providing the authoritative set of rules of procedure that any group needs in order to conduct business effectively in all cases not covered by its own special rules.

The manual is based on the rules and practices of the United States Congress adapted to the use of ordinary societies that are nonlegislative in character. It clearly and succinctly explains the methods of organizing and conducting meetings, the duties of officers, and the names of ordinary motions. It systematically describes each motion in detail, giving its object and effect, indicating whether it can be amended or debated, and, if debatable, the extent to which it opens the main question to debate. It gives the circumstances under which a motion can be made, and what other motions can be made while it is pending. Each rule is complete in itself, or refers to any section that in any way qualifies it. One unfamiliar with the entire work can thus refer safely to any special subject.

The manual is above all a reference book whose purpose is to provide a set of rules for adoption by city councils, corporations, clubs, societies, associations, assemblies, and occasional meetings and conventions. The best way to approach its study is first to learn the few elementary things that one must know in order to take the least part in a deliberative meeting and then to learn how to use the book to locate quickly the correct ruling or decision on any point that arises. The student is advised first to study sections 69 and 70 of Article XII, *Organization and Meetings*, then to study Article I, *How Business is Conducted in Deliberative Assemblies*. The student should commit to memory the table of the *Order of Precedence of Motions* and should be thoroughly familiar with the *Table of Rules Relating to Motions*, which answers at a glance 300 key questions on rulings. To facilitate familiarity with the overall design of the work a plan of the manual is provided, followed by a brief list of important definitions. The student should also study the index and practice using the book as a reference.

The book may then be studied in any sequence that the reader chooses to follow. The reader is recommended to master Article 33, to *Amend*. This is probably the most difficult and important topic in all of parliamentary law. Study each of the individual motions in the order in which they are treated, except the section devoted to *incidental motions*, which it is best to examine last. Look at the *Orders of the Day* in connection with the motions to *Postpone Definitely and Indefinitely*, because they are so intimately connected, the *Orders of the Day* being made by postponing to a certain time or by adopting a program. The subject of *Committees* should be studied in connection with the motion to *Commit*. To *Take from the Table* should be studied in connection with to *Lay on the Table*. While careful study is essential, the student should always remember *The New Robert's Rules of Order Revised* is a reference book. Learn how to find rulings quickly before trying to remember all of them. Keep the book on hand during meetings for such use.

Efficiency as a parliamentarian comes only with practice. No amount of theoretical knowledge alone will make a man or woman a good practical parliamentarian. A commitment to skillful leadership and a devotion to public life and service are qualities that motivated General Robert to prepare his *Rules of Order*. The student who masters this book through study and practice prepares to assume a leadership role in his or her group or community. Those who do will discover the individual accomplishment joined to a sense of responsibility to others that General Robert worked to promote.

Though the stresses, complexities, and problems of life in an advanced modern culture have alienated many of our fellow citizens, we remain fundamentally a democratic society under a government "of the people, by the people, and for the people." This is our heritage.

It is this that drives our public life. We may be critical of it, but we have the right to protest and be heard. We may be disappointed, but we have the opportunity to work for change. When better-organized professional, economic, or social interests distort public policy to their own selfish ends, we in turn can organize to balance the unhealthy weight of their influence. All adult members of our society have the right to participate in public debate and to cast their own judgment on public issues at the ballot box. We should never disparage these rights or take them for granted. We should always remember that, through our elected representatives, "we are the people assembled."

The history of the past decade has affirmed democracy in much of the world. The United States has made an enormous contribution to this, but we must remember that others among the family of nations have contributed as well. Our interventions in the world have not always been altruistic. Our domestic history has not always been unselfish and kind. The triumph of democratic government is not yet universal nor is it unproblematic. Some have recently seen in the triumph of democracy—or rather that of "democratic liberal capitalism"—an end of history, the achievement of a static perfection. It takes little hindsight, and much less foresight, to judge these claims absurd. Challenges have always confronted humanity. Now, more than ever, we are called upon to respond to problems that are global and critical. The gyre of debate has widened over a deep gulf. We are no longer merely engaged in political struggles among ourselves within local, state, or national boundaries. We are inextricably engaged in a world debate, and in a debate with nature itself. It remains to be seen whether the center can hold. That center must arise from the human individual gathered from the smallest group to that larger group that includes us all, and ultimately to one still larger that includes all life.

It is important, then, to understand our relationship in its larger context to that culture that General Henry M. Robert so well served in his crafting of a systematic manual of parliamentary procedure. Not all of us can act directly to assure the probity of the legal profession, the effectiveness of the medical establishment, the soundness of the banking system, or the accountability of political leaders to promote human rights and welfare, or to guarantee the environmental responsibility of industry, or to restrain the appetites of a consumption-oriented society. Many of us have associated to respond to these and other issues. But groups form with other motives that are equally legitimate, for business, social, literary, charitable, or other purposes. For all classes of groups, however motivated, a clear, complete, and accessible work on parliamentary law is needed. It is this need that the present edition of *Robert's Rules of Order* is designed to meet.

John Sherman
1993

A Note on Parliamentary Law from the 1915 edition of *Robert's Rules of Order*

A work on parliamentary law is needed, based, in its general principles, upon the rules and practices of Congress, but adapted, in its details, to the use of ordinary societies. Such a work should give not only the methods of organizing and conducting meetings, the duties of officers, and names of ordinary motions, but also a systematic statement in reference to each motion, as to its object and effect; whether it can be amended or debated; if debatable, the extent to which it opens the main question to debate; the circumstances under which it can be made, and what other motions can be made while it is pending. *Robert's Rules of Order* (published in 1876, slight additions being made in 1893) was prepared with a hope of supplying the above information in a condensed and systematic form, each rule being complete in itself, or giving references to every section that in any way qualifies it, so that a stranger to the work can refer to any special subject with safety.

The fact that a half million copies of these Rules have been published would indicate that there is a demand for a work of this kind. But the constant inquiries from all sections of the country for information concerning proceedings in deliberative assemblies that is not contained in *Rules of Order* seem to demand a revision and enlargement of the manual. To meet this want, the work has been thoroughly revised and enlarged, and, to avoid confusion with the old *Rules*, is published under the title *Robert's Rules of Order Revised.*

The object of *Rules of Order* is to assist an assembly to accomplish in the best possible manner the work for which it was designed. To do this it is necessary to restrain the individual somewhat, as the right of an individual, in any community, to do what he pleases, is incompatible with the interest of the whole. Where there is no law, but every man does what is right in his own eyes, there is the least of real liberty. Experience has shown the importance of definiteness in the law; and in this country, where customs are so slightly established and the published manuals of parliamentary practice so conflicting, no society should attempt to conduct business without having adopted some work upon the subject as the authority in all cases not covered by its own special rules.

While it is important that an assembly has good

rules, it is more important that it be not without some rules to govern its proceedings. It is much more important, for instance, that an assembly has a rule determining the rank of a motion to postpone indefinitely, than that it gives this motion the highest rank of all subsidiary motions except to lay on the table, as in the U.S. Senate; or gives it the lowest rank, as in the U.S. House of Representatives; or gives it equal rank with the previous question, to postpone definitely, and to commit, so that if one is pending none of the others may be moved, as under the old parliamentary law. This has been well expressed by one of the greatest of English writers on parliamentary law: "Whether these forms be in all cases the most rational or not is really not of so great importance. It is much more material that there should be a rule to go by than what the rule is; that there may be a uniformity of proceeding in business, not subject to the caprice of the chairman or captiousness of the members. It is very material that order, decency, and regularity be preserved in a dignified public body."

Plan of the Work and Definitions

The New Robert's Rules of Order is a modern revision of the classic manual of standard procedure for the conduct of business in organizations and deliberative assemblies that are not legislative in character. Based on the practices of the United States Congress, the rules are adapted to the needs of ordinary deliberative assemblies with short sessions and comparatively small quorums. The rules are complete. They may be altered or adapted to suit the special requirements of a particular organization or group. This manual contains a ***Table of Contents, Table of Rules, Part I, Part II, Notes,*** and ***Index.***

The ***Table of Contents*** clearly and systematically presents the arrangement of subjects treated in the manual.

The ***Order of Precedence of Motions*** and the ***Table of Rules*** enable anyone quickly to determine whether a motion is in order, or whether it may be debated, amended, reconsidered, requires a second, a two-thirds vote, or is in order when another member has the floor.

Part I systematically presents the ***Rules of Order.*** It shows how business is introduced in a deliberative assembly, and then follows it step by step until the vote is taken and announced. Section **10** shows which motion to use to accomplish certain objects, referring at the same time to the section where the motion is fully discussed. The motions are then classified into ***Privileged, Incidental, Subsidiary,*** and ***Main,*** and the general characteristics of each class are given. Each class is then taken up in order, beginning with the highest privileged motion. A section is devoted to each motion, including some that are unclassified. Each of these twenty-six sections is complete in itself, so that one unfamiliar with the work need not be misled in examining any particular subject. Cross-references to sections are given in brackets and **bold type.**

The following is stated in reference to each motion, except some of the incidental ones, the first six points being mentioned at the beginning of each section: ***(1) over which motions it takes precedence*** (i.e., over which motions when pending, it is in order to make and consider the motion); ***(2) to what motion it yields*** (i.e., what motions may be made and considered while this motion is pending); ***(3) whether it is debatable or not*** (all motions are debatable unless noted otherwise); ***(4) whether it can be amended or***

not; (5) when no subsidiary motion can be applied to the motion [see ***Adjourn,* 17,** for an example. The motion to ***adjourn*** cannot be ***laid on the table, postponed, committed,*** or ***amended,*** etc.]; ***(6) the vote required for its adoption,*** when it is not a majority; ***(7) the form of making the motion when peculiar; (8) the form of stating and putting the question when peculiar; (9) the object of the motion when not apparent;*** and ***(10) the effect of the motion if adopted,*** whenever it could possibly be misunderstood.

Part II describes the methods of organizing and conducting different kinds of meetings, giving the words used by the chair and speakers in making and putting various motions. A few pages are also devoted to the legal rights of deliberative assemblies and ecclesiastical tribunals, and to the trial of their members. To obtain a correct understanding of the methods of conducting business in deliberative assemblies, the beginner will find it very useful to read sections **69–71** in connection with sections **1–10.**

The ***Notes*** give the congressional procedure when *Robert's Rules* departs from it, and need only be consulted for this purpose.

The ***Index*** refers to pages, not sections. It is introduced with suggestions for the best methods to find anything in the rules.

Accepting a report is the same as ***adopting*** it, and should not be confused with ***receiving*** a report, which is allowing it to be presented to the assembly.

Assembly. This term is used for the deliberative assembly, and should be replaced in motions, etc., by the proper name of the body, as society, club, church, board, convention, etc. The ***Chair*** means the presiding officer, whether temporary or permanent. The terms ***Congress*** and ***H.R.***, when used in this Manual, refer to the U.S. House of Representatives.

Meeting and ***Session.*** Meeting is used in this Manual for the assembling of the members of a deliberative body for any length of time during which they do not separate for longer than a few minutes, as the morning or the evening meeting of a convention. In a society with rules providing for regular meetings every week, or month, etc., each of these regular meetings is a separate session. A called or special meeting is a distinct session. Should a regular or special meeting adjourn to meet at another time, the adjourned meeting is a continuation of the session, not a separate one; the two meetings constitute one session. In the case of a convention holding a meeting every year or two, or rather a series of meetings lasting several days, the entire series of meetings constitute one session. [See **63**.]

Pending and ***Immediately Pending.*** A question is said to be pending when it has been stated by the chair and has not yet been disposed of either permanently or temporarily. When several questions are pending, the one last stated by the chair, and therefore the one to be first disposed of, is said to be the immediately pending question.

A ***Main motion*** is one that is made to bring before the assembly any particular subject. No main motion can be made when another motion is pending.

A ***Subsidiary motion*** is one that may be applied to a main motion, and to certain other motions, for the purpose of modifying them, delaying action upon them, or otherwise disposing of them.

Privileged motions are such that, while having no relation to the pending question, are of such urgency or importance as to require them to take precedence over all other motions.

An ***Incidental motion*** is one that arises out of another question that is pending or has just been pending, and must be decided before the pending question, or before other business is taken up. Incidental motions have no fixed rank but take precedence over the questions out of which they arise, whether those questions are *main, subsidiary,* or *privileged.*

The ***Previous Question*** does **not** refer, as its name implies, to the previous question. It is the name given to the motion to close debate and to take the vote at once on the immediately pending question and such other questions as are specified in the motion.

A ***Substitute*** is an amendment where an entire resolution or section, or one or more paragraphs, is struck out and another resolution or section, or one or more paragraphs, is inserted in its place.

Plurality, Majority, and ***Two-thirds Vote***. In an election a candidate has a plurality when he or she has a larger vote than any other candidate; a candidate has a majority when he or she has more than half the votes cast, ignoring blanks. In an assembly a plurality never elects except by virtue of a rule to that effect. A majority vote when used in these rules means a majority of the votes cast, ignoring blanks, at a legal meeting, a quorum being present. A two-thirds vote is two-thirds of the votes cast as just described. For an illustration of the difference between a two-thirds vote of the members present, and a vote of two-thirds of the members, see *Two-thirds Vote,* **48**.

Order of Precedence of Motions

The list below shows the rank of the ordinary motions, the motions lowest in rank at the bottom of the list, and the highest at the top. When any one of them is immediately pending, the motions above it in the list are in order, and those below are out of order. Those marked (⅔) require a two-thirds vote for their adoption. The others require only a majority.

Undebatable:	***Fix the Time to which to Adjourn*** (when privileged)*†	Privileged
Undebatable:	***Adjourn*** (when privileged)†	Privileged

---

*These can be amended. The others cannot be amended.

†The first three motions are not always privileged. To ***Fix the Time to which to Adjourn*** is privileged only when made while another question is pending, and in an assembly that has made no provision for another meeting on the same or the next day. To ***Adjourn*** loses

Undebatable: ***Take a Recess*** (when privileged)*† ....: Privileged
Undebatable: ***Raise a Question of Privilege*** ....: Privileged
Undebatable: ***Call for the Orders of the Day*** ....: Privileged

Undebatable: ***Lay on the Table***
Undebatable: ***Previous Question*** (2/3) ....: Subsidiary
Undebatable: ***Limit or Extend Limits of Debate*** (2/3)* ....: Subsidiary

Debatable: ***Postpone to a Certain Time**** ....: Subsidiary
Debatable: ***Commit or Refer**** ....: Subsidiary
Debatable: ***Amend**** ....: Subsidiary
Debatable: ***Postpone Indefinitely*** ....: Subsidiary
Debatable: ***A Main Motion****

---

its privileged character and is a main motion if in any way qualified, or if its effect, if adopted, is to dissolve the assembly without any provision for its meeting again. To ***Take a Recess*** is privileged only when made while other business is pending.

Section in Rules of Order, Revised	Explanation of the Table:	Debatable	Debate Confirmed to Pending Question	Can Be Amended	Subsidiary Motions Can Be Applied	Can Be Reconsidered	Requires Only A Majority Vote	Must Be Seconded	Out of Order When Another Has Floor
S#	TABLE OF RULES RELATING TO MOTIONS	01	02	03	04	05	06	07	08
17	Adjourn (when privileged) 1	-★	—	-★	-★	-★	—	—	—
54	Adopt (Accept or Agree to) a Report	—	—	—	—	—	—	—	—
67	Adopt Constitution, By-Laws, Rules of Order	—	—	—	—	-2	—	—	—
67	Adopt Standing Rules	—	—	—	—	—	—	—	—
33	Amend 3	-4	—	—	—	—	—	—	—
33	Amend an Amendment	-4	—	-★	—	—	—	—	—

Explanation of the Table: The numbers in the left-hand column indicate the sections where the motions are discussed. The rules at the head of the 8 columns to the right apply to all original main motions and to all cases except where a star (★) or a number indicates that the motion is an exception to these rules. The star shows that the exact opposite of the rule at the head of the column applies to the motion. Two-thirds ⅔ is shown (in column six) where a two-thirds vote is required. A number refers to a note that explains the extent of the exception. For example, the table shows that §28 of the manual treats the motion **to lay on the table,** that this motion is **undebatable** and cannot **be amended,** that **no subsidiary motion can be applied to it,** and that it **cannot be reconsidered.** The fact that the 4 other columns have no stars or figures shows that the rules at the head of these columns apply to this motion, to Lay on the Table, just as to original main motions.

Table continued on next page

S#	TABLE OF RULES RELATING TO MOTIONS (continued)	01	02	03	04	05	06	07	08
68	Amend Constitution, By-laws, Rules of Order	—	—	—	—	-2	-5	—	—
67	Amend Standing Rules	—	—	—	—	—	-6	—	—
21	Appeal, relating to Indecorum, etc 7	-★	—	-★	—	—	—	—	-★
21	Appeal, all other cases	—	—	-★	—	—	—	—	-★
33	Blanks, Filling	—	—	-★	—	—	—	-★	—
32	Commit or Refer, or Recommit	—	—	—	—	-8	—	—	—
30	Debate, to Close, Limit, or Extend 9	-★	—	—	—	—	-2/3	—	—
25	Division of the Assembly	-★	—	-★	-★	-★	—	-★	-★
24	Division of the Question	-★	—	—	—	-★	—	10	10
16	Fix the Time to which to Adjourn 1	11	—	—	—	—	—	—	—
57	Informal Consideration of a Question	—	—	-★	—	-2	—	—	—
28	Lay on the Table	-★	—	-★	-★	-★	—	—	—
21	Leave to Continue Speaking after Indecorum	-★	—	-★	-★	—	—	—	—
11	Main Motion or Question	—	—	—	—	—	—	—	—
26	Nominations, to Make	—	—	-★	—	-★	—	-★	—
26	Nominations, to Close	-★	—	—	—	-★	-2/3	—	—
26	Nominations, to Reopen	-★	—	—	—	-2	—	—	—
23	Objection to Consideration of a Question	-★	—	-★	-★	-2	12	-★	-★
21	Order, Questions of	-★	—	-★	-★	-★	—	-★	-★
20	Order, to Make a Special	—	—	—	—	—	-2/3	—	—

20	Orders of the Day, to Call for	-★	—	-★	-★	-★	—	-★	-★
20	Order of the Day, when pending	—	—	—	—	—	—	—	—
27	Parliamentary Inquiry	-★	—	-★	-★	-★	—	-★	-★
31	Postpone Definitely, or to Certain Time	—	—	—	—	—	—	—	—
34	Postpone Indefinitely	—	-★	-★	—	13	—	—	—
29	Previous Question 14	-★	—	-★	-★	15	-2/3	—	—
19	Privilege, to Raise Questions of	-★	—	-★	-★	-★	—	-★	-★
19	Privilege, Questions of, when pending	—	—	—	—	—	—	—	—
27	Reading Papers	-★	—	-★	-★	—	—	—	—
18	Recess, to Take a (when privileged) 1	11	—	—	—	-★	—	—	—
36	Reconsider 16	-4	17	-★	—	-★	—	—	-★
37	Rescind or Repeal	—	-★	—	—	-2	18	—	—
33	Substitute (same as Amend)	—	—	—	—	—	—	—	—
22	Suspend the Rules	-★	—	-★	-★	-★	-2/3	—	—
35	Take from the Table	-★	—	-★	-★	-★	—	—	—
22	Take up a Question out of its Proper Order	-★	—	-★	-★	-★	-2/3	—	—
25	Voting, Motions relating to	-★	—	—	—	—	—	—	—
27	Withdraw a Motion, Leave to	-★	—	-★	-★	-2	—	-★	—

Table of Rules Relating to Motions Answering 300 Questions in Parliamentary Practice

Key to the Table of Rules Relating to Motions:

[S#] Section in ***The New Rules of Order.***
[01] ***Debatable.***
[02] ***Debate Confined to Pending Questions.***
[03] ***Can be Amended.***
[04] ***Subsidiary Motions can be Applied.***
[05] ***Can be Reconsidered.***
[06] ***Requires only a Majority Vote.***
[07] ***Must be Seconded.***
[08] ***Out of Order when Another has Floor.***

Explanation of the Table of Rules Relating to Motions:

Everyone participating in the meetings of a deliberative assembly should know and be able quickly to refer to the ***Order of Precedence of Motions*** and the ***Table of Rules.*** The tables contain an epitome of parliamentary law. The ***Order of Precedence of Motions*** should be memorized. It contains all of the privileged and subsidiary motions, 12 in number, arranged in their order of rank, and shows for each motion whether it can be debated or amended, what vote it requires, and under what circumstances it can be made.

In the ***Table of Rules*** the headings of the 8 columns are rules or principles that apply to all original main motions. They should be memorized. They are ***(1) Original Main Motions are debatable; (2) debate must be confined to the immediately pending question; (3) they can be amended; (4) all subsidiary motions can be applied to them; (5) they can be reconsidered; (6) they require only a majority vote for their adoption; (7) they must be seconded;*** and ***(8) they are not in order when another has the floor.*** Whenever any of the 44 motions in the Table differs from a main motion in regard to any of these rules, the exception is indicated by a star (★) or a number in the proper column opposite that motion. A star shows that the exact opposite of the rule at the head of the column applies to the motion. A number refers to a note that explains the extent of the exception. A blank shows that the rule at the head of the column applies, and therefore that the motion is in this respect exactly like a main motion. Some of the motions are followed by figures not in the columns. These figures refer to notes giving useful information in regard to these motions.

The ***Table of Rules*** is constructed on the theory that it is best to learn the general principles of parliamentary law as applied to original main motions, and then to note where each other motion is an exception to these general rules. For example, the motion to ***postpone definitely, or to a certain time*** has no stars or figures opposite it. It is therefore subject to all of the above 8 rules just as any main motion. To ***postpone indefinitely*** has two stars and the number 13 opposite it. This shows that the rules at the head of these three columns do not apply to this motion. The first star shows that debate is not confined to the motion to postpone indefinitely, but that the main motion is also open to debate; the second star shows that the motion to postpone indefinitely cannot be amended; and the number 13 refers to a note that shows that a negative vote on the motion cannot be reconsidered.

As already stated, a star shows that the motion, instead of being subject to the rule at the head of the column, is subject to a rule exactly the opposite. Stars in the various columns, therefore, mean that the motions are subject to the following rules: ***(1) undebatable; (2) opens main questions to debate; (3) cannot be amended; (4) no subsidiary motion can***

be applied; (5) cannot be reconsidered; (6) requires a two-thirds vote; (7) does not require to be seconded; and ***(8) is in order when another has the floor.***

Notes to the Table of Rules Relating to Motions

[1] See last footnote to the ***Order of Precedence of Motions.***

[2] An affirmative vote on this motion cannot be reconsidered.

[3] An Amendment may be made *(a)* by *inserting* (or *adding*) words or paragraphs; *(b)* by *striking out* words and paragraphs; *(c)* by *striking out certain words* and *inserting others;* or *(d)* by *substituting* one or more paragraphs for others, or an entire resolution for another, on the same subject.

[4] Undebatable when the motion to be amended or reconsidered is undebatable.

[5] Constitutions, By-laws, and Rules of Order before adoption are in every respect main motions and may be amended by majority vote. After adoption they require previous notice and two-thirds vote for amendment.

[6] Standing Rules may be amended at any time by a majority vote if previous notice has been given and by a two-thirds vote without notice.

[7] An Appeal is undebatable only when made while an undebatable question is pending, or when relating to indecorum, to transgressions of the rules of speaking, or to the priority of business. When debatable, only one speech from each member is permitted. A tie vote sustains the decision of the chair.

[8] Cannot be reconsidered after the committee has taken up the subject, but by two-thirds vote the committee at any time may be discharged from further consideration of the question.

[9] These motions may be moved whenever the immediately pending question is debatable, and apply to it alone, unless otherwise specified.

[10] If resolutions or propositions relate to different subjects that are independent of each other, they must be divided on the request of a single member, which can be made when another has the floor. If they relate to the same subject and yet each part can stand alone, they may be divided only on a regular motion and vote.

[11] Undebatable if made when another question is before the assembly.

[12] The objection can be made only when the question is first introduced, before debate. A two-thirds vote must be opposed to the consideration in order to sustain the objection.

[13] A negative vote on this motion cannot be reconsidered.

[14] The Previous Question may be moved whenever the immediately pending question is debatable or amendable. The questions upon which it is moved should be specified; if not specified, it applies only to the immediately pending question. If adopted it cuts off debate and at once brings the assembly to a vote on the immediately pending question and such others as are specified in the motion.

[15] Cannot be reconsidered after a vote has been taken under it.

[16] The motion to reconsider can be made while any other question is before the assembly, and even while another has the floor, or after it has been voted to adjourn, provided the assembly has not been declared adjourned. It can be moved only after the day, or the day after, the vote that it is proposed to reconsider was taken, and by one who voted with the prevailing side. Its consideration cannot interrupt business unless the motion to be reconsidered takes precedence over the immediately pending question. Its rank is the same as that of the motion to be reconsidered, except that it takes precedence of a general order, or of a motion of equal rank with the motion to be reconsidered, provided their consideration has not actually begun.

[17] Opens the main question to debate, when the main question is debatable.

[18] Rescind is under the same rules as to amend something already adopted. See notes to 2, 5, and 6, above.

Additional Rules: Incidental Motions. Motions that are incidental to pending motions take precedence over them and must be acted upon first [see **13** for a list of these motions].

No privileged or subsidiary motion can be laid on the table, postponed definitely or indefinitely, or committed. When the main question is laid on the table, etc., all adhering subsidiaries go with it.

PART I:

Rules of Order

Article I: How Business is Conducted in Deliberative Assemblies

1. INTRODUCTION OF BUSINESS
2. WHAT PRECEDES DEBATE
3. OBTAINING THE FLOOR
4. MOTIONS AND RESOLUTIONS
5. SECONDING MOTIONS
6. STATING THE QUESTION
7. DEBATE
8. SECONDARY MOTIONS
9. PUTTING THE QUESTION AND ANNOUNCING THE VOTE
10. PROPER MOTIONS TO USE TO ACCOMPLISH CERTAIN OBJECTS

1. Introduction of Business. After an assembly is organized [**69**, **70**, **71**], the motion of a member or the presentation of a communication brings business before it. A formal motion is often unnecessary.

Motions are rarely made to receive reports of committees or communications to the assembly, but a regular motion is required if any member demands one. The presiding officer can introduce a question without waiting for a motion.

2. What Precedes Debate. Three steps are required before any subject is open to debate: a member who has obtained the floor makes a motion; the motion is seconded (with certain exceptions); the presiding officer, also called the ***chair,*** states the motion. Only the chair can put a motion before the assembly, either ruling it out of order or stating the question on it, thus presenting it for consideration and action as the ***immediately pending question.*** If several questions are pending—for instance, a resolution, an amendment, and a motion to postpone—the last one stated by the chair is the ***immediately pending question.***

After a motion is made, no debate or other motion is in order until the chair states the motion or rules it out of order. Members may suggest modifications to it. The mover may modify the motion without the seconder's consent; the seconder may then withraw his or her second, or may even entirely withdraw it *before* the chair states the question on it. Afterward, the mover can only modify or withdraw it with the assembly's consent [**27**(c)]. Informal discussion before the question is stated can save time, but the chair must prevent abuse of this privilege, not allowing it to run into debate.

3. Obtaining the Floor. A member must ***obtain the floor*** before making a motion or addressing the assembly in debate. After the floor has been yielded, the member rises and addresses the presiding officer by his or her official title, ***Mr./Madame President*** or ***Mr./Madame Chair.***[1] The member should state his or her name if unknown to the chair. If the member is entitled to the floor (discussed below), the chair ***recognizes*** the member and assigns the floor by announcing his or her name. These procedures may be observed less formally in small meetings. If a member rises before the floor is yielded, or is standing at the time, he or she does not have the right to obtain the floor if anyone else rises afterward and addresses the chair. It is out of order to be standing when another has the floor. A member who violates the rules cannot claim precedence.

The member has precedence who first rises to address the chair after the floor is yielded. It is sometimes in the interest of the assembly that the floor be assigned to a member who was not the first to rise. Three classes of such cases arise: *(1) when a debatable question is immediately pending; (2) when an undebatable question is immediately pending; (3) when no question is pending*. The following principles should guide the chair in assigning the floor.

(1) When a debatable question is immediately pending. ***(1a)*** Although another has risen first and addressed the chair, the member upon whose motion the immediately pending question was brought before the assembly is entitled to recognition if he or she has not already spoken on the question. The member who reports or submits a committee report is entitled to preference. When a question is taken from the table, the member who moved to do so enjoys preference. When a motion is made to reconsider, the member who moved to reconsider has precedence, this member not necessarily the one who calls up the motion. ***(1b)*** No member who has already had the floor in debate on the immediately pending question is again entitled to the floor for debate on the same question when the floor is claimed by a member who has not spoken on it. ***(1c)*** If no other criteria for precedence apply, the assembly's interests are best served when the floor is allowed to alternate between the friends and enemies of a measure.

(2) The mover of an undebatable immediately pending question enjoys no preference. The floor should be assigned in accordance with the principles given in ***3b.***

(3) When no question is pending. ***(3a)*** When one of a series of motions has been disposed of, and no question is actually pending, the next of the series has the right of way. Even if another member rises first and addresses the chair, the chair should recognize the member who introduced the series to make the next motion. No other main motion is in order until the assembly disposes of the series. A motion may be introduced to lay a question on the table. This motion is designed to lay a question aside temporarily in order to take up more urgent business. The member who moves to set the question aside is entitled to the floor to introduce the urgent business, but only if he or she claims the floor immediately. When a member moves to reconsider a vote for the announced purpose of amending the motion, if the vote is reconsidered, he or she must be recognized in preference to others in order to move the amendment. ***(3b)***: If no question is pending and no series of motions has been started that has not been disposed of, the member who rises to move to reconsider a vote, or to call up a previously made motion to reconsider, or to take a question from the table when it is in order is entitled to the floor in preference to another who rises slightly beforehand to introduce a main motion. The member who rises afterward must state his or her purpose. Preference is first given to members who rise to make motions to reconsider and last to those who rise to move to take from the table. When a motion has been adopted to appoint a committee for a certain purpose or to refer a subject to a committee, no new subject (except a privileged one) can be introduced until the assembly has decided on the composition of the committee, the manner of its selection, and the instructions to be given to it. The member who makes the motion to appoint a committee, or to refer a subject to one, enjoys no preference. The member should include in his or her first motion all motions he or she wishes to make.

Any two members may appeal the chair's decision in assigning the floor. One makes the appeal; the other seconds it.[2] When in doubt as to who is entitled to the floor, the chair may allow the assembly to decide the issue by a vote.

When a member rises to claim the floor, or is assigned the floor, it is the chair's duty to protect this member from the disorder of calls for the question, or of motions to adjourn or to lay the question on the table. A member not recognized by the chair can make a motion only by general consent. If it is made and anyone afterwards rises to claim the floor, thus showing that general consent has not been given, the chair should not recognize the motion.

In Order When Another Has the Floor: After a member is assigned the floor, he or she can only be interrupted by ***(a)*** *a motion to reconsider;* ***(b)*** *a point of order;* ***(c)*** *an objection to the consideration of the question;* ***(d)*** *a call for the orders of the day* (when they are not conformed to); ***(e)*** *a question of privilege;* ***(f)*** *a request or a demand that the question be divided* (when it consists of more than one independent resolution on different subjects); ***(g)*** *a parliamentary inquiry;* or ***(h)***

a request for information (when it requires immediate answer). After a member entitled to the floor begins to speak, these eight cases are used only when their application is urgent. These interruptions do not deprive the speaker of the right to the floor. After the matters have been dealt with, the chair returns the floor to the speaker. When a member submitting a committee report or offering a resolution hands it to the secretary to be read, the member does not yield the floor. After the reading is finished and the chair states the question, no one can make a motion until the member submitting the report or offering the resolution has a reasonable opportunity to claim the floor. If the member makes no motion to accept or adopt the resolution when submitting the report, he or she should resume the floor as soon as the report is read to make the proper motion to carry out the recommendations, after which he or she is entitled to the floor for debate as soon as the question is stated.

4. Motions and Resolutions. A motion is a proposal that the assembly take an action or express certain views. To make a motion a member obtains the floor and says, **"I move that"** (the equivalent of saying **"I propose that"**), and then states the action he or she proposes. A member thus ***"moves"*** that a resolution be adopted, amended, or referred to a committee, or that a vote of thanks be extended, etc. Every resolution should be in writing. The presiding officer has a right to require any main motion, amendment, or instructions to a committee to be in writing. A main motion of any length or importance is usually written in the form of a ***resolution***; that is, beginning with the words ***Resolved, That,*** the word ***Resolved*** being underscored (printed in *italics*) and followed by a comma, and the word ***That*** beginning with a capital ***T.*** If the word ***Resolved*** is replaced by the words ***I move,*** the resolution becomes a motion. A resolution is always a main motion. In some sections of the country the word ***resolve*** is frequently used instead of ***resolution.*** In assemblies with paid employees, instructions given to employees are called ***orders*** instead of ***resolutions,*** and the enacting word ***Ordered*** is used instead of ***Resolved.***

When a member seeks adoption of a resolution, after having obtained the floor, he or she says, **"I move the adoption of the following resolution,"** or **"I offer the following resolution,"** which he or she reads and hands to the chair. The reasons for the resolution, if it is desired to give them, are usually stated in a ***preamble,*** each clause of which constitutes a paragraph beginning with ***Whereas.*** The preamble is always amended last, as changes in the resolution may require changes in the preamble. In moving the adoption of a resolution the preamble is not usually referred to, as it is included in the resolution. But when the previous question is ordered on the resolution before the preamble has been considered for amendment, it does not apply to the preamble, which is then open to debate and amendment. The preamble should never contain a period. Each paragraph should close with a comma or semicolon, followed by ***and,*** except the last paragraph, which should close with the word ***therefore,*** or ***therefore, be it.*** A resolution should avoid periods wherever possible. If periods are necessary, it is usually better to separate it into a series of resolutions, in which case the resolutions may be numbered by preceding them with the figures 1, 2, etc.; or it may retain the form of a single resolution with several paragraphs, each beginning with ***That.*** If prefered, these paragraphs may be numbered by placing ***First, Second,*** etc., just before the word ***That.*** The following illustrates the form for giving the reasons for a resolution:

Whereas, We consider that suitable recreation is a necessary part of a rational education system; and
Whereas, There is no public ground in this village where our school children can play; therefore,
Resolved, That a committee of five be appointed by the chair to present these resolutions to the village authorities and to urge upon them prompt action in the matter.

As a general rule, a member can make two motions at a time only by general consent. But he or she may combine the motion to suspend the rules with the motion for whose adoption it was made, and the motion to reconsider a resolution and its amendments. A member also may offer a resolution and at the same time move to make it a special order for a specified time.

5. Seconding Motions. Generally, with the exceptions given below, every motion should be seconded. This rule prevents waste of time in considering a question that only one person favors. In routine motions little attention is paid to it. The chair, when certain that a motion is generally approved, may proceed without waiting for a second. However, any member may then make a point of order that the motion has not been seconded. The chair is then obliged to proceed formally and call for a second. When a motion is not immediately seconded, it is better for the chair to ask, **"Is the motion seconded?"** In a large hall, to be sure that everyone has heard the motion, the chair should repeat it before calling for a second. After a motion has been made no other motion is in order until the chair has stated the question on this motion, or has declared, after a reasonable opportunity has been given for a second, that the motion has not been seconded, or has ruled it out of order. The chair should always state the facts. Only in small assemblies can the chair assume that members know what the motion is and that it has not been seconded.

A motion is seconded when a member says, **"Mr./Madame Chair, I second the motion,"** or **"I second it."** This is done without obtaining the floor; in small assemblies without rising.

The following do not require a second[3]: *Question of Privilege, to raise a* **[19]**; *Questions of Order* **[21]**; *Objection to the Consideration of a Question* **[23]**; *Call for Orders of the Day* **[20]**; *Call for Division of the Question* (under certain circumstances) **[24]**; *Call for Division of the Assembly* (in voting) **[25]**; *Call up Motion to Reconsider* **[36]**; *Filling Blanks* **[33]**; *Nominations* **[33]**; *Leave to Withdraw a Motion* **[27]**; *Inquiries of any kind* **[27]**.

6. Stating the Question. When a motion is made and seconded, the chair should either immediately rule it out of order or ***state the question***; i.e., state the exact question that is before the assembly for its consideration and action. The chair may do this in various ways according to the nature of the question: "It is moved and seconded that the following resolution be adopted [reading the resolution]." "It is moved and seconded to adopt the following resolution." "Mr. A offers the following resolution [read], the question is on its adoption." "It is moved and seconded to amend the resolution by striking out the word 'very' before the word 'good.'" "The previous question has been demanded [or, moved and seconded] on the amendment." "It is moved and seconded that the question be laid on the table." "It is moved and seconded that we adjourn." [The form of stating the question is shown under each motion, if there is any peculiarity in it]. If the question is debatable or amendable, the chair should immediately ask, "Are you ready for the question?" If no one rises, the chair should put the question to vote **[9]**. If the question cannot be debated or amended, the chair puts the question to vote immediately after stating it.

7. Debate. After the chair states a question, it is before the assembly for consideration and action. All resolutions, reports of committees, communications to the assembly, all amendments proposed to them, and all other motions except the Undebatable Motions noted in **45**, may be debated until final action is taken on them, unless by a two-thirds vote (two-thirds of the votes cast, a quorum present) the assembly decides to dispose of them without debate. In the debate each member has the right to speak twice on the same question on the same day (except on an appeal), but cannot make a second speech on the same question as long as any member who has not spoken on that question desires the floor. No one can speak longer than ten minutes at a time without permission of the assembly.

Debate must be limited to the merits of ***immediately pending question***; i.e., the last question stated by the chair that is still pending. In a few cases, however, the main question is also open to debate **[45]**. Speakers must address their remarks to the presiding officer, be courteous in their language and deportment, and avoid all personal comments, never alluding to the officers or the other members by name where possible to avoid it, nor to the motives of members. [See *Debate*, **42,** and *Decorum in Debate*, **43.**]

8. Secondary Motions. To assist in the proper disposal of the question various ***subsidiary motions*** **[12]** are used, such as to *amend*, to *commit*, etc., and for the time being the subsidiary motion replaces the resolution or motion and becomes the ***immediately pending question.*** While these are pending, a question incidental to the business may arise, a question of order for instance. This ***incidental*** **[13]** question interrupts the business and becomes the immediately pending question until it is disposed of. All of these may be superseded by ***privileged motions*** **[14]**. These are of such supreme importance that they may interrupt all other questions. The motions that may be made while the original motion is pending are sometimes referred to as ***secondary motions.*** The proper uses of many of these are shown in **10.**

9. Putting the Question and Announcing the Vote.[4] When the debate seems to have closed, the chair asks again, **"Are you ready for the question?"** If no one rises the chair ***puts the question*** (i.e., takes the vote on the question), calling first for the affirmative and then for the negative vote. In putting the question, the chair should state clearly the question that the assembly is to decide. If the question is on the adoption of a resolution, it should be read again unless it has been read recently. The question is put in a way similar to this: "The question is on the adoption of [or agreeing to] the resolution [which the chair reads]; those in favor of the resolution say aye; those opposed say no. The ayes have it and the resolution is adopted." Or, "The noes have it, and the resolution is lost." Or, "It is moved and seconded that an invitation be extended to Mr. Amory to address our club at its next meeting. Those in favor of the motion will rise; be seated; those opposed to the measure will rise. The affirmative has it and the motion is adopted [or carried]." Or, if the vote is by show of hands, the question is put and the vote announced in a form similar to this: "It has been moved and seconded to lay the resolution on the table. Those in favor of the motion will raise the right hand; those opposed will signify [or manifest] it in the same way [or manner]. The affirmative has it [or, The motion is adopted, or carried] and the resolution is laid on the table." It is a necessary part of putting the question that the vote should always be announced. The assembly is not assumed to know the result of the vote until the chair announces it. No vote goes into affect until it is announced. After the result of the vote is announced the chair should state the next business in order, as in the following example of putting the question on an amendment: "The question is on amending the resolution by inserting the word 'oak' before the word 'desk.' Those in favor of the amendment say aye; those opposed say no. The ayes have it and the amendment is adopted. The question is now [or recurs] on the resolution as amended, which is as follows [read the resolution as amended]. Are you ready for the question?" To avoid confusion, the chair should always state the business next in order after every vote is announced, and the exact question before the assembly whenever a motion is made. The vote should always be taken first by voice (***viva voce***) or by *show of hands* (a method often used in small assemblies), except when a motion requires a two-thirds vote. A rising vote then should first be taken, as when a division is demanded. [See *Voting*, **46**]. The form of putting the question is given under each motion, whenever peculiar.

10. Proper Motions to Use to Accomplish Certain Objects. Below are given the common motions according to the objects attained by their use, followed by summaries of the differences between the motions placed under each object and of the circumstances under which each should be used. They include all of the ***Subsidiary Motions*** [12] designed for properly disposing of a question pending before the assembly, the three motions designed to bring again before the assembly a question that has been acted upon or temporarily laid aside, and the motion designed to bring before another meeting of the assembly a main question that has been voted on in an unusually small or unrepresentative meeting. In general, the adoption of motions requires only a majority vote (a majority of the votes cast, a quorum being present). Motions to suppress or limit debate, to prevent the consideration of a question, or without notice to rescind action previously taken require a two-thirds vote **[48]**. The (numbers) and (letters) correspond to the (numbers) and (letters) in the statement of differences that follows it. The [bracketed numbers] refer to the sections where the motions are fully treated.

The Common Motions Classified According to Their Objects: (1) To Modify or Amend: (1a) *Amend* **[33]**; ***(1b)*** *Commit or Refer* **[32]**. ***(2) To Defer Action: (2a)*** *Postpone to a Certain Time* **[31]**; ***(2b)*** *Make a Special Order* (*2/3 Vote*) **[20]**; ***(2c)*** *Lay on the Table* **[28]**. ***(3) To Suppress or Limit Debate (2/3 Vote): (3a)*** *Previous Question (to close debate now, 2/3 Vote)* **[29]**; ***(3b)*** *Limit Debate* (*2/3 Vote*) **[30]**. ***(4) To Suppress the Question: (4a)*** *Objection to Its Consideration (2/3 Vote)* **[23]**; ***(4b)*** *Previous Question and Reject*

Question [29]; ***(4c)*** *Postpone Indefinitely* [34]; ***(4d)*** *Lay on the Table* [28]. ***(5) To Consider a Question a Second Time: (5a)*** *Take from the Table* [35]; ***(5b)*** *Reconsider* [36]; ***(5c)*** *Rescind* [37]. ***(6) To Prevent Final Action on a Question in an Unusually Small or Unrepresentative Meeting: (6a)*** *Reconsider and have entered on the Minutes* [36].

(1) To Modify or Amend. (1a) Amend [33]: When a resolution or motion is improperly worded or requires any change to obtain the assembly's approval, and the changes required can be made in the assembly, the proper motion to make is to amend by ***inserting, adding, striking out,*** by ***striking out and inserting,*** or by ***substituting*** one or more paragraphs for those in the resolution. ***(1b) Commit or Refer*** [32]: If this is time consuming, if many changes are required or more information is needed before the assembly can act intelligently, it is usually better to refer the question to a committee.

(2) To Defer Action. (2a) Postpone to a Certain Time [31]: To delay further consideration of a question until a certain hour, so that when that time arrives, as soon as the pending business is disposed of, it shall have the right of consideration over all questions except special orders and a reconsideration, the proper motion to make is to ***postpone to a certain time***. This is also the proper motion to make simply to defer action to another day. Because the motion if adopted can neither interrupt the pending question when the appointed time arrives nor suspend any rule, only a majority vote is required for its adoption. A question postponed to a certain time cannot be taken up before the appointed time except by suspending the rules, requiring a two-thirds vote. ***(2b) Make a Special Order (⅔ Vote)*** **[20]**: To appoint for the consideration of a question a certain time when it may interrupt any pending question except one relating to adjournment or recess, a question of privilege or a special order that was made before it was, the proper course is to move ***"that the question be made a special order for,"*** etc., specifying the day or hour. As this motion, if adopted, suspends all rules that interfere with the consideration of the question at the appointed time, it requires a two-thirds vote for its adoption. A special order cannot be considered before the appointed time except by suspending the rules, requiring a two-thirds vote. ***(2c) Lay on the Table*** **[28]**: If a member wishes to lay a question aside temporarily with the right to take it up at any moment when business of this class, or unfinished or new business is in order, the proper motion to use is to ***lay the question on the table.*** When laid upon the table a majority vote may take it up at the same or the next session [see **35**].

(3) To Suppress or Limit Debate (⅔ Vote). (3a) Previous Question (to close debate now, ⅔ Vote) **[29]**: To close debate immediately and bring the assembly at once to a vote on the pending question or questions, the proper course is to move, or demand, or call for the previous question on the motions upon which it is desired to close debate. The motion or demand for the previous question should always specify the motions upon which the member wishes to order the previous question. If no motions are specified, the previous question applies only to the immediately pending question and requires a two-thirds vote for its adoption. After it has been adopted, privileged and incidental motions may be made, or the pending questions may be laid on the table, but no other subsidiary motion can be made nor is any debate allowed. If it is lost the debate is resumed. ***(3b) Limit Debate (⅔ Vote)*** [**30**]: To limit the number or length of speeches, or the time allowed for debate, the proper method is to move that the speeches or debate be limited as desired, or that the debate be closed and the vote be taken at a specified time. These motions require a two-thirds vote for their adoption. They are in order, like the previous question, when any debatable question is immediately pending.

(4) To Suppress the Question. In a deliberative assembly only a two-thirds vote can suppress a legitimate question without free debate. If two-thirds of the assembly are opposed to the consideration of the question then the following methods can be used to suppress it. ***(4a) Objection to Its Consideration (⅔ Vote)*** [**23**]: To prevent any consideration of the question, the proper method is to ***object to its consideration*** before it has been discussed or any other motion stated. It may therefore interrupt a member who has the floor before the debate has begun. It requires no second. A two-thirds negative vote is required to prevent the consideration. ***(4b) Previous Question and Reject Question*** [29]: After the question has been considered the proper way to suppress it immediately is to close debate by ordering the previous question, which requires a two-thirds vote, and then to vote down the question. ***(4c) Postpone Indefinitely*** [34]: Another method of suppressing a question is ***to postpone it indefinitely*** (equivalent to rejecting it). This motion is debatable and opens the main question to debate. It is only useful in giving another opportunity to defeat the resolution should this one fail, because, if the motion to postpone indefinitely is adopted, the main question is dead for the session, and, if it is lost, the main question is still pending and its enemies have another chance to kill it. When the motion to postpone indefinitely is pending and immediate action is desired, the previous question must be moved as in ***4b*** above. ***(4d) Lay on the Table*** [28]: A fourth method often used for suppressing a question is to ***lay it on the table***, though this is an unfair use of the motion, except in bodies like Congress where the majority must have power to suppress any motion immediately, as otherwise they could not transact business. In ordinary societies, where the pressure of business is not as great, it is better policy for the majority to be fair to the minority and use the proper motions for suppressing a question without allowing full debate, all of which require a two-thirds vote. Unless the enemies of a motion have a large majority, laying it on the table is not a safe way of suppressing it, because its friends, by watching their opportunity, may find themselves in a majority and take it from the table and adopt it, as shown in ***5a***.

(5) To Consider a Question a Second Time. (5a) Take from the Table [35]: When a question has not been voted on, but has been laid on the table, a majority may take it from the table and consider it at any time when no other question is before the assembly and when business of that class, or unfinished or new business, is in order during the same session, or at the next session in ordinary societies having regular meetings as often as quarterly. ***(5b) Reconsider*** [36]: If a motion has been adopted, or rejected, or postponed indefinitely, and afterwards one or more members have changed their views from the prevailing to the losing side, and it is thought by further discussion the assembly may modify or reverse its action, the proper course is for one who has voted with the prevailing side to move to ***reconsider*** the vote on the question. This can be done on the day the vote to be reconsidered is taken, or on the next succeeding day of the same session. ***(5c) Rescind*** [37]: If a main motion, including questions of privilege and orders of the day, has been adopted, rejected, or postponed indefinitely, and no one is both able and willing to move to reconsider the vote, the question can be brought up again during the same session only by moving to ***rescind*** the motion. To ***rescind*** may be moved by any member, but if notice of it was not given at a previous meeting it requires a two-thirds vote or a vote of the majority of the enrolled membership. If the question cannot be reached by calling up the motion to reconsider that was made at the previous session, the resolution or other main motion may be rescinded in the same way at any future session if it had been adopted, or it may be introduced again if it had been rejected or postponed indefinitely. A by-law, or anything else that requires a definite notice and vote for its amendment, requires the same notice and vote to rescind it.

(6a) To Prevent Final Action on a Question in an Unusually Small or Unrepresentative Meeting. If an important main motion is adopted, lost, or postponed indefinitely at a small or unrepresentative meeting, when it is clear that the action is contrary to the views of the majority, the proper course to pursue is for a member to vote with the prevailing side and then move ***to reconsider the vote and have it entered on the minutes.*** The motion to reconsider, in this form, can be made only on the day the vote was taken that it is proposed to reconsider, and the reconsideration cannot be called up on that day; thus an opportunity is given to notify absent members. [See *Motion to Reconsider*, **36.**]

Article II: General Classifications of Motions

For convenience motions may be classified as follows:

11. MAIN OR PRINCIPAL MOTIONS
12. SUBSIDIARY MOTIONS
13. INCIDENTAL MOTIONS
14. PRIVILEGED MOTIONS
15. SOME MAIN AND UNCLASSIFIED MOTIONS

11. Main or Principal Motions are made to bring any particular subject before the assembly for its consideration. A Main Motion takes precedence over nothing. It cannot be made when any other question is before the assembly. It yields to all privileged, incidental, and subsidiary motions, any of which can be made while a main motion is pending. Main motions are debatable and subject to amendment. Subsidiary motions [12] can be applied to them. When a main motion is laid on the table, or postponed to a certain time, it carries with it all pending subsidiary motions.

If a main motion is referred to a committee it carries

with it only the pending amendments. Amendments generally require for their adoption only a majority of the votes cast. However, amendments to constitutions, by-laws, and rules of order already adopted, all of which are main motions, require a two-thirds vote for their adoption, unless the by-laws, etc., specify a different vote for their amendment. The motion to rescind action previously taken requires a two-thirds vote, or a vote of the majority of the entire membership, unless previous notice of the motion has been given.

Main Motions may be subdivided into ***Original Main Motions*** and ***Incidental Main Motions***. An ***Original Main Motion*** brings a new subject (generally in the form of a resolution) before the assembly for its action. An ***Incidental Main Motion*** is a main motion that is incidental or relates to the business of the assembly or to its past and future action, for example a committee's report on a resolution referred to it. A motion to accept or adopt the report of a standing committee on a subject not referred to it is an original main motion, but a motion to adopt a report on a subject referred to a committee is an incidental main motion. The introduction of an original main motion can be prevented by a two-thirds vote sustaining an objection to its consideration [23]. This objection must be made just after the main motion is stated and before it is discussed. An objection to its consideration cannot be applied to an incidental main motion, but a two-thirds vote can immediately suppress it by ordering the previous question **[29]**. This is the only difference between the two classes of main motions. The following are some of the most common ***Incidental Main Motions:*** *Accept or Adopt a Report* upon a subject referred to a committee **[54]**; *Adjourn at,* or *to,* a future time **[17]**; *Adjourn,* if qualified in any way, or to adjourn when the effect is to dissolve the assembly with no provision for its reconvening **[17]**; *Appoint the Time and Place for the next meeting,* if introduced when no business is pending **[16]**; *Amend the Constitution, By-laws, Standing Rules, or Resolutions,* etc., already adopted **[68]**; *Ratify* or *Confirm* action taken **[39]**; *Rescind* or *Repeal* action taken **[37]**. All of these motions are essentially main motions, and are treated as such, though they may appear otherwise.

A question of privilege ranks high and can interrupt a pending question. However, a question of privilege is treated as a main motion when it interrupts business and is itself pending. Incidental and subsidiary motions can be applied to it. An order of the day, even though a special order, is treated in the same way when it is pending. This is also true of a question that is reconsidered.

No motion is in order when it conflicts with the constitution, by-laws, standing rules, or resolutions of the assembly. All such motions are null and void, even if adopted. Before introducing such motions, the constitution or by-laws must be amended, or the conflicting standing rule or resolution must be amended or rescinded. Any motion is out of order that conflicts with a resolution previously adopted by the assembly at the same session, or with one that has been introduced and has not been finally disposed of. If it is not too late the proper course is to reconsider **[36]** the vote on the motion previously adopted, and then to amend it to express the desired idea. If it cannot be reconsidered, then the old resolution may be rescinded by a two-thirds vote, after which the new motion can be introduced. Alternatively, notice can be given and the old motion may be rescinded by a majority vote at the next meeting. In ordinary societies, where the quorum is a small percentage of the membership and the meetings are as frequent as quarterly, no resolution that conflicts with one adopted at a previous session should be entertained until the old one has been rescinded. This requires a two-thirds vote unless proper notice has been given **[37]**.

12. Subsidiary Motions are applied to other motions in order best to dispose of them. By means of subsidiary motions the original motion may be modified, action on it may be postponed, or it may be referred to a committee to investigate and report, etc. Subsidiary motions may be applied to any main motion. When made they supersede the main motion and must be decided before the main motion can be acted upon. Only the motion to amend, and those motions that close or limit or extend the limits of debate, can be applied to subsidiary, incidental (except an appeal in certain cases), or privileged motions. Subsidiary motions, except to *lay on the table the previous question,* and to *postpone indefinitely* may be amended. The motions affecting the limits of debate may be applied to any debatable question regardless of its privilege. These require a two-thirds vote to be adopted. All those of lower rank than those affecting the limits of debate are debatable. The rest are not. The motion to amend anything that has already been adopted, as by-laws or minutes, is not a subsidiary motion but is a main motion and can be laid on the table or have applied to it any other subsidiary motion without affecting the by-laws or minutes, because the latter are not pending.

The following list gives the subsidiary motions in the order of their precedence. The first one has the highest rank. When one of them is the immediately pending question every motion before it is in order, and every one after it is out of order. ***Subsidiary Motions:*** *Lay on the Table* **[28]**; *The Previous Question* **[29]**; *Limit or Extend Limits of Debate* **[30]**; *Postpone Definitely, or to a Certain Time* **[31]**; *Commit or Refer, or Recommit* **[32]**; *Amend* **[33]**; *Postpone Indefinitely* **[34]**.

13. Incidental Motions arise out of another question that is pending. They therefore take precedence over the question out of which they arise and must be decided before it. They can also apply to a question that has just been pending. In this case they should be decided before any other business is taken up. Incidental motions yield to privileged motions, and generally to the motion to lay on the table. They are undebatable, except an appeal under certain circumstances as shown in **21**. They can be amended only when they relate to the division of a question, to the method of considering a question, to the methods of voting, or to the time when nominations or the polls shall be closed. No subsidiary motion can be applied to any of them except to *amend* and a debatable appeal. Whenever it is stated that all incidental motions take precedence over a certain motion, the incidental motions referred to are only those that are legitimately incidental at the time they are made. Thus, incidental motions take precedence over subsidiary motions, but the incidental motion to object to the consideration of a question cannot be made while a subsidiary motion is pending, because the objection is only legitimate against an original main motion just after it is stated, before it has been debated or there has been any subsidiary motion stated. The following are the most common incidental motions: *Questions of Order and Appeal* [**21**]; *Suspension of the Rules* [**22**]; *Objection to the Consideration of a Question* [**23**]; *Division of a Question, and Consideration by Paragraph or Seri-*

atim **[24]**; *Division of the Assembly, and Motions Relating to Methods of Voting, or to Closing or to Reopening the Polls* **[25]**; *Motions Relating to Methods of Making, or to Closing or to Reopening Nominations* **[26]**; *Requests Growing out of Business Pending or that has just been pending (a Parliamentary Inquiry, a Request for Information, for Leave to Withdraw a Motion, to Read Papers, to be Excused from a Duty, or for any other Privilege)* **[27]**.

14. Privileged Motions, while not relating to the pending question, are of such importance that they take precedence over all other questions. Due to this high privilege, they are undebatable. No subsidiary motion can be applied to them, except the motions to fix the time to which to adjourn, and to take a recess, which may be amended. But after the assembly has actually taken up the orders of the day or a question of privilege, debate and amendment are permitted and the subsidiary motions may be applied just as to any main motion. Given in their order of precedence, the ***Privileged Motions*** are: *Fix the Time to which to Adjourn* (if made while another question is pending) **[16]**; *Adjourn* (if unqualified and if it has not the effect to dissolve the assembly) **[17]**; *Take a Recess* (if made when another question is pending) **[18]**; *Raise a Question of Privilege* **[19]**; *Call for the Orders of the Day* **[20]**.

15. Some Main and Unclassified Motions. Two main motions (to *rescind* and to *ratify*) and several motions that cannot be conveniently classified as either Main, Subsidiary, Incidental, or Privileged, and that are in common use, are explained in the sections indicated where their privileges and effects are given. They are *Take from the Table* **[35]**; *Reconsider* **[36]**; *Rescind* **[37]**; *Renewal of a Motion* **[38]**; *Ratify* **[39]**; *Dilatory, Absurd, or Frivolous Motions* **[40]**; and *Call of the House* **[41]**.

Article III: Privileged Motions

16. FIX THE TIME TO WHICH THE ASSEMBLY SHALL ADJOURN
17. ADJOURN
18. TAKE A RECESS
19. QUESTIONS OF PRIVILEGE
20. GENERAL AND SPECIAL ORDERS AND A CALL FOR THE ORDERS OF THE DAY

[See **14** *for a list and the general characteristics of these motions.]*

16. Fix the Time to which the Assembly shall Adjourn.[1] This motion is privileged only while another question is pending and in an assembly that has made no provision for another meeting on the same or the next day. The time fixed cannot be beyond the time of the next meeting. If made in an assembly that already has provided for another meeting on the same or the next day, or when no question is pending, this is a main motion. Like other main motions, it may be debated and amended and have applied to it the other subsidiary motions. Whenever the motion is referred to in these rules, the privileged motion is meant unless otherwise noted. When privileged, this motion takes precedence over all others. It is in order even after it has been voted to adjourn, provided the chair has not declared the assembly adjourned. It can be amended and a vote on it can be reconsidered. When the assembly has no fixed place for its meetings, this motion should include the place as well as the time for the next meeting, both of which are subject to amendment. When the assembly meets at the time to which it adjourned, the meeting is a continuation of the previous session. Thus, if the Annual Meeting is adjourned to meet on another day, the adjourned meeting is a legal continuation of the Annual Meeting **[63]**. The form of the motion is "**I move that we adjourn** [or **stand adjourned**] **to three P.M. tomorrow.**"

17. Adjourn. The motion to adjourn (when unqualified) is always a privileged motion except when (for lack of provision for a future meeting) its effect if adopted would be to dissolve the assembly permanently. The privileged motion to ***adjourn*** takes precedence over all others except the privileged motion to ***fix the time to which to adjourn,*** to which it yields. It cannot be debated or amended or have any other subsidiary motion **[12]** applied to it. It may be withdrawn, but a vote on it cannot be reconsidered.

When the motion to adjourn is qualified in any way, or when its effect is to dissolve the assembly without making any provision for holding another meeting of the assembly, it loses its privilege and becomes a main motion. As a main motion it is debatable and amendable. Any of the subsidiary motions may be applied to it.

The motion to adjourn can be repeated if there has been any intervening business, even if this is simply the continuation of debate. The assembly may decline to adjourn in order to hear a speech or to take a vote. It must therefore have the privilege of renewing the motion to adjourn after any progress in business or debate. This high privilege can be disruptive if abused. The chair must refuse to entertain the motion when it is clearly made for obstructive purposes, for instance just after the assembly has voted it down and there is no subsequent indication of the assembly's wish to adjourn. [See *Dilatory Motions,* **40.**]

Only a member who has the floor can make the motion to adjourn. When made by one who has not risen and been recognized, it can be entertained only by general consent. It cannot be made when the assembly is voting, or verifying a vote, but it is in order before a vote taken by ballot has been announced. In such cases the ballot vote should be announced as soon as business is resumed. Whenever counting ballots takes any length of time, the assembly may adjourn, appointing beforehand a time for the next meeting, or still better taking a recess as explained in the next section. No appeal, question of order, or inquiry should be entertained after the motion to adjourn has been made, unless its decision is necessary before adjournment. If the assembly refuses to adjourn, then it would be in order.

Before putting the motion to adjourn, the chair should be sure that no important matters have been overlooked. All announcements should be made before taking the vote, or at least before announcing it. If a matter requires action before adjournment, the fact should be stated and the mover requested to withdraw the motion to adjourn. Although the motion to adjourn is undebatable, the assembly should be informed of business requiring attention before adjournment. Members should remain seated until the chair declares adjournment.

An adjournment ***sine die*** (without day) closes the session. If there is no provision for reconvening the assembly, the adjournment dissolves it. If provision has been made to hold another meeting, it simply closes the session. In an assembly, as a convention, which meets regularly only once during its life, but whose by-laws provide for calling special meetings, an adjournment *sine die* means only the ending of the regular session of the convention, which, however, may be reconvened as provided in the by-laws. If called to meet again, the assembly meets as a body already organized.

In committees where no provision has been made for future meetings, an adjournment is always at the call of the chair unless otherwise specified. When a special committee, or the committee of the whole, completes the business referred to it, instead of adjourning, it *rises* and reports. This is equivalent to adjournment without day.

The ***Effect upon Unfinished Business*** of an adjournment, unless the assembly has adopted rules to the contrary, is as follows. ***(a)*** When the adjournment does not close the session **[63]**, the business that it interrupted is the first in order after the reading of the minutes at the next meeting and is treated just as if there had been no adjournment, an adjourned meeting being legally the continuation of the meeting of which it is an adjournment. ***(b)*** When the adjournment closes a session[2] in an assembly having regular sessions as often as quarterly, the unfinished business should be taken up, where it was interrupted, at the next succeeding session before any new business is considered. However, in a body elected either wholly or in part for a definite time, unfinished business falls to the ground with the expiration of the term for which the membership or any part of it was elected. ***(c)*** When the adjournment closes a session in an assembly that does not meet as often as quarterly, or when the assembly is an elective body, and this session ends the term of a portion of the members, the adjournment puts an end to all business unfinished at the close of the session. The business may be introduced at the next session, just as if it had never been before the assembly.

18. Take a Recess.[3] This motion is essentially a combination of the two preceding. It yields to these and takes precedence over all other motions. If made when other business is before the assembly, it is a privileged motion and is undebatable and can have no subsidiary motion applied to it except amend (the proposed length of the recess can be amended). It takes effect immediately. A motion to take a recess made when no business is before the assembly, or to take a recess at a future time, has no privilege. It is treated as any other main motion. A recess is an intermission in the day's proceedings, for meals, for counting the ballots, etc. In meetings such as conventions lasting for several days a recess is sometimes taken over an entire day. When a recess is provided for in the order of exercises or program, the chair announces it when the time arrives and says the assembly stands adjourned, or in recess, to the specified hour. The assembly by a two-thirds vote can postpone the time for taking a recess or adjournment. When the hour has arrived to which the recess was taken, the chair calls the assembly to order and the business proceeds just as if no recess had been taken. If the recess was taken after a vote had been taken and before it was announced, the first business is the announcement of the vote. The intermissions in the proceedings of a day are termed recesses, whether the assembly voted to take a recess or whether it simply adjourned, having beforehand adopted a program or rule providing for the hours of meeting. When an assembly has frequent short regular meetings not lasting over a day, and an adjourned meeting is held on another day, the interval between the meetings is not referred to as a recess.

19. Questions of Privilege. Questions relating to the rights and privileges of the assembly, or to any of its members, take precedence over all other motions except the three preceeding relating to adjournment and recess, to which they yield. If the question requires immediate action, it may interrupt a member's speech, for example, when the speech is inaudible. After a member begins to speak, he or she should only be interrupted if the matter is urgent. It is in order for another member to raise a question of privilege before a member begins to speak, even though he or she has been assigned the floor. A member rising for this purpose should not wait to be recognized, but should immediately say, "Mr./Madame Chair," and, catching the chair's eye, should add, "I rise to a question of privilege affecting the assembly," or "I rise to a question of personal privilege." The chair directs the member to state his or her question, and then decides whether it is one of privilege or not. Any two members may appeal this decision. If the chair decides it to be a question of privilege, but not of such urgency to interrupt the speaker, the speaker should be allowed to conclude and then should immediately assign the floor to the member who raised the question of privilege to make a motion if one is necessary. Once made and stated, this becomes the immediately pending question and is open to debate and amendment and the application of all other subsidiary motions just as any main motion. Its high privilege extends only to giving it the right to consideration in preference to any other question except one relating to adjournment or recess, and, in urgent cases, the right to interrupt a member while speaking. It cannot interrupt voting or verifying a vote. When the question of privilege is disposed of, business is resumed exactly where it was interrupted. If a member had the floor at the time the question of privilege was raised, the chair reassigns the floor to this member.

Questions of privilege may relate to the privileges of the assembly or only of a member, the former having the precedence if the two compete. Questions of personal privilege must relate to one as a member of the assembly, or else relate to charges against his or her character that if true would incapacitate him or her for membership. The following questions relate to the privileges of the assembly: those relating to the organization of the assembly; to the comfort of its members, as the heating, lighting, ventilation, etc., of a hall, and freedom from noise and other disturbance; to the conduct of its officers and employees; to the punishing of a member for disorderly conduct or other offence; to the conduct of reporters for the press; or to the accuracy of published reports of proceedings.

Besides questions of privilege, privileged questions include a call for the orders of the day and the privileged motions relating to adjournment and recess. This distinction between privileged questions and questions of privilege should be remembered.

20. Orders of the Day.[4] ***A Call for the Orders of the Day*** is a demand that the assembly conform to its program or order of business. It can *only* be made when no other privileged motion [14] is pending and the order of business is not respected. It requires no second. It is in order when another has the floor, even though it interrupts a speech. It is out of order to call for the orders of the day when there is no variation from the order of business. The orders of the day cannot be called for when another question is pending, provided there are no special orders made for that time or an earlier time. General orders cannot interrupt a question actually under consideration. The call must simply be for the orders of the day, not for a specified one, as the latter has no privilege. When the time arrives for which a special order has been made, a call for the orders of the day takes precedence over everything except the other privileged motions, i.e. those relating to adjournment and recess, and questions of privilege, to which it yields. If made when no question is pending, the call is in order even when another has the floor and has made a main motion, provided the chair has not stated the question. Until the time of actually taking up the general orders for consideration, this call yields to a motion to reconsider, or to a calling up of a previously made motion to reconsider. A call for the orders of the day cannot be debated or amended, or have any other subsidiary motion applied to it.

It is the chair's duty to announce in its proper order the business to come before the assembly. When this is done, there is no reason to call for the orders of the day. The chair sometimes fails to notice that the time assigned for a special order has arrived, or thinks that the assembly is so interested in the pending question that it does not wish yet to take up the special order assigned for that time, and therefore delays announcing it. Any member then may call for the orders of the day, thus compelling the chair either to announce the order or to put the question "Will the assembly proceed to the orders of the day?" Because a refusal to take up the orders of the day at the appointed time is an interference with the order of business similar to suspending the rules, a negative vote of two-thirds is required to prevent proceeding to them. If the assembly refuses to proceed to them, the orders cannot again be called for until the pending business is disposed of.

If continuation of the discussion of the pending question is desired when the orders of the day are announced or called for, someone should move that the time for considering the pending question be extended a certain number of minutes. Because this changes the order of business or program, a two-thirds vote is required for the adoption of this motion. After the order has been announced and the question is actually pending, it is debatable and may be amended or have any other subsidiary motion applied to it just as any other main motion. The orders of the day cannot be laid on the table or postponed collectively. However, when an order has been actually taken up, it may by majority vote be laid on the table, postponed, or committed, so that, if there is no other order to interfere, the consideration of the question previously pending will be resumed. Whenever the orders of the day are disposed of, the consideration of the interrupted business is taken up where it was interrupted by the call for the orders of the day.

When one or more subjects have been assigned to a particular day or hour by postponing them to or making them special orders for that day or hour, or by adopting a program or order of business, they become the orders of the day for that day or hour. They can be considered before that time only by a two-thirds vote. They are divided into ***General Orders*** and ***Special Orders*** The latter always takes precedence over the former. A ***General Order*** is usually made by simply postponing a question to a certain day or hour, or after a certain event. It does not suspend any rule, and therefore cannot interrupt business. After the appointed hour has arrived, it has preference, when no question is pending, over all other questions except special orders and reconsideration. It can only be considered before the appointed time by a reconsideration or by a two-thirds vote. When the order of business provides for orders of the day, questions simply postponed to a meeting without specifying the hour come up under that head. If no provision is made for orders of the day, then such postponed questions come up after the disposal of the business pending at the previous adjournment, and after the questions on the calendar that were not disposed of at the previous meeting.

General Orders are an order of business that specifies the order in which, but not the time when, business shall be transacted, together with the postponed questions. This order can be changed only by general consent or by suspending the rules by a two-thirds vote. If all of this business is not disposed of before adjournment, it becomes ***unfinished business*** and is treated as such. [See *The Effect Upon Unfinished Business of an Adjournment*, **17.**]

Because general orders cannot interrupt the consideration of a pending question, a general order made for an earlier hour, if not disposed of in time, may interfere with a general order made before it. Therefore, general orders must take precedence among themselves in the order of the times to which they were postponed, regardless of when the general order was made. If several are appointed for the same time, then they take precedence in the order in which they were made. If several appointed for the same time were made at the same time, then they take precedence in the order in which they were arranged in the motion making the general order.

To ***Make a Special Order*** requires a two-thirds vote, because it suspends all rules that interfere with its consideration at the specified time, except those relating to motions for adjournment or recess, to questions of privilege, or to special orders made before it was made. A pending question is made a special order for a future time by ***postponing it and making it a special order*** for that time. [See *Postpone Definitely or to a Certain Time,* **31.**] If the question is not pending, the motion to make it a special order for a certain time is a main motion, debatable, amendable, etc. The member who wishes to make it a special order should obtain the floor when nothing is pending, and business of that class or new business is in order, and say, "I move that the following resolution be made the special order for [specifying the time]," and then read the resolution and hand it to the chair. Or he or she may adopt this form: "I offer the following resolution, and move that it be made a special order for the next meeting." Where a committee has been appointed to submit a revision of the constitution, the following resolution may be adopted: "Resolved, That the revision of the constitution be made the special order for Thursday morning and thereafter until it is disposed of."

Program. Another way of making special orders is by adopting a program, or order of business, in which is specified the hour for taking up each topic. It is usual to adopt a program or order of business for conventions in session for several days. Since delegates and invited speakers come from a distance, it is important that the program be followed strictly. After its adoption by the assembly, only a two-thirds vote can alter it. When the hour assigned to a certain topic arrives, the chair puts to vote any questions pending and announces the topic for the hour. The form of the program implies that the time assigned to each topic is all that can be allowed. If anyone moves to lay the question on the table, to postpone it to a certain time, or to refer it to a committee, the chair should recognize the motion and immediately put it to a vote without debate. Should anyone move to extend the time allotted the pending question, it should be decided instantly without debate. A two-thirds vote is required for the extension. Because it is unfair to the next topic, an extension is rarely desirable. It is extremely discourteous to call for the orders of the day when an invited speaker exceeds his or her time. The chair should have an understanding with invited speakers as to how and when the expiration of their time will be indicated. If a speaker continues beyond this, the chair should rise and declare the time expired.

A ***series of Special Orders made by a single vote*** is treated like a program. At the hour assigned to a particular subject it interrupts the question assigned to the previous hour. By a majority vote, the discussion of the pending topic can be continued at another time by laying it on the table or postponing it until after the close of the interrupting question.

Special Orders made at different times for specified hours sometimes come into conflict. The special order that was first made takes precedence over all made afterward, even when the latter were made for an earlier hour. No special order can be made that interferes with one made beforehand. They can be arranged in the desired order by reconsidering the vote making the first special order. For example, after a special order has been made for 3 P.M., one is made for 2 P.M., and still later one is made for 4 P.M.; if the 2 P.M. order is pending at 3 P.M., the order for 3 P.M., having been made first, interrupts it and continues, if not previously disposed of, beyond 4 P.M., regardless of the special order for that hour. When it, the 3 P.M. order, is disposed of, the special order for 2 P.M. is resumed even if it is after 4 P.M., because the 2 P.M. order was made before the 4 P.M. order. The only exception to this rule is in the case of the hour fixed for recess or adjournment. When that hour arrives the chair announces it and declares the assembly adjourned or in recess, even though there is a special order pending that was made before the hour for recess or adjournment was fixed. When the chair announces the hour, anyone can move to postpone the time for adjournment, or to extend the time for considering the pending question. These motions are undebatable and require a two-thirds vote.

Special Orders when only the day or meeting is specified. Subjects are often made special orders for a meeting without specifying an hour. If the order of business provides for orders of the day, they come up under that head, taking precedence over general orders. If there is no provision for orders of the day, they come up under unfinished business—i.e., before new business. If there is no order of business, then they may be called up at any time after the minutes are disposed of.

The Special Order for a Meeting. A subject is sometimes made *the* special order for a meeting, as for Tuesday morning in a convention, in which case the chair announces it as the pending business immediately after the disposal of the minutes. This particular form is used when it is desired to devote an entire meeting, or as much of it as is necessary, to considering a special subject, the revision of the by-laws, for example. This form of a special order should take precedence over the other forms of special orders. It is debatable and amendable.

Article IV: Incidental Motions

21. QUESTIONS OF ORDER AND APPEAL
22. SUSPENSION OF THE RULES
23. OBJECTION TO THE CONSIDERATION OF A QUESTION
24. DIVISION OF A QUESTION, AND CONSIDERATION BY PARAGRAPH OR BY SERIATIM
25. DIVISION OF THE ASSEMBLY, AND MOTIONS RELATING TO METHODS OF VOTING, OR TO CLOSING AND REOPENING THE POLLS
26. MOTIONS RELATING TO METHODS OF MAKING OR TO CLOSING OR TO REOPENING NOMINATIONS
27. REQUESTS GROWING OUT OF BUSINESS PENDING OR THAT HAS JUST BEEN PENDING, AS A PARLIAMENTARY INQUIRY, A REQUEST FOR INFORMATION, FOR LEAVE TO WITHDRAW A MOTION, TO READ PAPERS, TO BE EXCUSED FROM A DUTY, OR REQUEST FOR ANY OTHER PRIVILEGE

21. Questions of Order and Appeal. A ***Question of Order*** takes precedence over the pending question from which it rises. It is in order when another has the floor and can interrupt a speech or the reading of a report. It does not require a second and cannot be amended or have any other subsidiary motion applied to it. It yields to privileged motions and the motion to lay upon the table. The chair decides it without debate.

Before rendering a decision, the chair may request the advice of experienced members. To avoid the appearance of debate, members should usually remain seated when giving this advice. If still in doubt, the chair may submit the decision to the assembly in this manner: "Mr. A raises the point of order that the amendment just offered [state the amendment] is not germane to the resolution. The chair is in doubt, and submits the question to the assembly. The question is 'Is the amendment germane to the resolution?'" Because the assembly's decision cannot be appealed, this question is open to debate whenever an appeal would be, as when the chair decides the question and that decision is appealed. It is therefore debatable except when it relates to indecorum, to transgression of the rules of speaking, or to the priority of business. It is not debatable when it is made during a division of the assembly, or while an undebatable question is pending. The question is put thus: "As many as are of opinion that the amendment is germane [or that the point is well taken] say aye; as many as are of a contrary position say no. The ayes have it, the amendment is in order, and the question is on its adoption." If the negative vote is larger, it is announced thus: "The noes have it, the amendment is out of order, and the question is on the adoption of the resolution." Whenever the presiding officer decides a question of order, he or she has the right without leaving the chair to state the reasons for his or her decision. Any two members have the right to appeal the decision. One makes the appeal. The other seconds it.

It is the chair's duty to enforce the rules and orders of the assembly without debate or delay. Any member who notices the violation of a rule may insist upon its enforcement. This is called raising a question or point of order because the objecting member puts to the chair the question of there having been a breach of order. The member rises and says, "Mr./Madame Chair, I rise to a point of order." The speaker (the member who has the floor when another member rises to a point of order) immediately sits down, and the chair requests the risen member to state the point of order. This the member does and resumes his or her seat. The chair decides the point. If this decision is not appealed and the speaker is not guilty of a serious breach of decorum, the chair permits the speaker to continue. If a speaker's remarks are decided to be improper, he or she cannot continue without the assembly's consent. [See *Decorum in Debate*, **43**.]

The question of order must be raised *when* the breach of order occurs. After a motion has been discussed, it is too late to question whether it is in order, and too late for the chair to rule it out of order. It is never too late to raise a point of order against a motion when it violates the laws, constitution, by-laws, or standing rules of the organization, or is contrary to fundamental parliamentary principles so that if adopted it would be null and void. When simply a case of improper language used in debate, the chair usually calls the speaker to order or a member says, "I call the lady/gentleman to order." The chair decides whether the speaker is in or out of order, and proceeds as before.

Appeal. Except when another appeal is pending, any decision of the chair may be appealed. The appeal must be made at the time of the ruling, *before* any debate or business intervenes. An appeal is in order while another member has the floor. An answer to a parliamentary inquiry is not a decision and cannot be appealed. A question of order may be raised while an appeal is pending. The chair decides this peremptorily, as this decision cannot be appealed. However, the question of the correctness of the ruling can be brought up afterwards when no other business is pending. An appeal yields to privileged motions and to the motion to lay on the table.

The ***effect of subsidiary motions*** is as follows. An appeal cannot be amended. If reversal of the appealed decision would have no affect on the consideration of or action on the main question, the main question does not adhere to the appeal; its consideration is resumed as soon as the appeal is laid on the table, postponed, etc. But if the ruling affects the consideration of or action on the main question, then the main question adheres to the appeal, and when the appeal is laid on the table or postponed, the main question goes with it. If an appeal is made to the chair's decision that a proposed amendment is out of order, and the appeal is laid on the table, it would be absurd to come to final action on the main question and then afterward reverse the decision of the chair and take up the amendment when there is no longer a question to amend. The vote on an appeal may be reconsidered.

An appeal cannot be debated when it relates simply to indecorum, to violations of the rules of speaking, to the priority of business, or if made during a division of the assembly or when the immediately pending question is undebatable. It is debatable in all other cases. Only the chair, who may at the close of the debate answer the arguments against the decision, is allowed to speak more than once. Whether debatable or not, the presiding officer when stating the question on the appeal may without leaving the chair state the reasons for his or her decision.

When a member wishes to appeal the decision of the chair he or she rises as soon as the decision is made, even when another member has the floor. Without waiting to be recognized, the member says, "Mr./Madame Chair, I appeal the decision of the chair." If this appeal is seconded, the chair should clearly state the question at issue and the reasons for the decision if he or she thinks it necessary. The chair then states the question thus: "The question is, 'Shall the decision of the chair stand as the judgement of the assembly [or society, club, etc.]?'" or, "Shall the decision of the chair be sustained?" To put the question he or she would say, "Those in the affirmative say aye," and after the affirmative vote has been taken would say, "Those in the negative say no. The ayes have it and the decision of the chair is sustained [or stands as the judgment of the assembly]." Or, "The noes have it and the decision of the chair is reversed." In either case the chair immediately announces what is before the assembly as the result of the vote. A tie vote sustains the chair. If the chair is a member of the assembly, he or she may vote to make it a tie, on the principle that the decision of the chair stands until reversed by a majority. The announcement of a vote is not a decision of the chair. A member who doubts the correctness of the announcement cannot appeal, but should call for a ***Division*** **[25]**.

22. Suspension of the Rules.[1] The motion to suspend the rules may be made whenever no other question is pending. It may be made while a question is pending if for a purpose related to that question. It yields to all the privileged motions (except a call for the orders of the day), to the motion to lay on the table, and to incidental motions arising out of itself. It is undebatable and cannot be amended. It can have no other subsidiary motion applied to it. A vote on it cannot be reconsidered. A motion to suspend the rules for the same purpose can be renewed at the same meeting only by unanimous consent. It may be renewed after an adjournment, even if the next meeting is held the same day.

When the assembly wishes to do something that cannot be done without violating its own rules, but does not conflict with its own constitution or by-laws, or with the fundamental principles of parliamentary law, it ***suspends the rules that interfere with*** the proposed action. The object of the suspension must be specified. Nothing else can be done under the suspension. The rules that can be suspended are those relating to priority of business, to business procedure, or to admission to the meetings, etc. These are usually found under the heads of rules of order. Sometimes societies include in their by-laws some rules relating to the transaction of business without any apparent intention of giving these rules any greater weight than is possessed by other rules of their class. These may be suspended just as if they were rules of order. A ***standing rule*** as defined in **67** may be suspended by a majority vote. Sometimes the term ***standing rule*** is applied to what are strictly rules of order, which then, like rules of order, require a two-thirds vote for their suspension. Nothing that requires previous notice and a two-thirds vote for its amendment can be suspended by less than a two-thirds vote.

No rule can be suspended when the negative vote is as large as the minority protected by that rule. General consent or a unanimous vote cannot suspend a rule protecting absentees. For instance, a rule requiring notice of a motion to be given at a previous meeting cannot be suspended by a unanimous vote, because it protects absentees who do not give their consent. A rule requiring officers to be elected by ballot cannot be suspended by a unanimous vote, because the rule protects a minority of one from exposing his or her vote. Nor can this result be accomplished by voting that the ballot of the assembly be cast by the secretary or anyone else, because this does away with secrecy, the essential principle of the ballot, is a suspension of the by-law, and practically allows a *viva voce* vote. To allow the suspension of a by-law that cannot be suspended under these rules, the by-laws must provide for its suspension.

The *Form* of this motion is to "suspend the rules that interfere with," etc., stating the object of the suspension as, "the consideration of a resolution on . . ." This resolution is offered immediately after the rules are suspended. The chair recognizes for this purpose the member who moved to suspend the rules.

To consider a question that has been laid on the table and cannot be taken up because that class of business is not then in order, or to consider a question that has been postponed to another time or that is in the order of business for another time, a motion may be made thus, "I move to suspend the rules and take up [or consider] the resolution . . ." When the object is not to take up a question for discussion but to adopt it without debate, the motion is made thus: "I move to suspend the rules and adopt [or agree to] the following resolution [which is then read]." Or, "I move to suspend the rules, and adopt [or agree to] the resolution on . . ." The same form may be used in a case like this: "I move to suspend the rules, and admit to the privileges of the floor members of sister societies." This motion merely admits them to the hall.

Instead of moving formally to suspend the rules, it is more usual to ask for general consent to do the particular business that is out of order. As soon as the request is made, the chair inquires if there is any objection. If not, the chair directs the member to proceed just as if the rules had been suspended by a formal vote. [See *General Consent,* **48.**]

23. Objection to the Consideration of a Question. An objection may be made to the consideration of any original main motion, and to no others, provided it is made before there is any debate or before any subsidiary motion is stated. It may thus be applied to resolutions as well as to petitions and to communications that are not from a superior body. It cannot be applied to incidental main motions **[11]** such as amendments to by-laws, or to reports of committees on subjects referred to them, etc. It is similar to a question of order in that it can be made when another has the floor and does not require a second. Just as the chair can call a member to order, so upon his or her own responsibility can the chair put this question if he or she thinks it advisable. It cannot be debated, amended, or have any other subsidiary motion applied to it. It yields to privileged motions and to the motion to lay on the table. A negative but not an affirmative vote on the consideration may be reconsidered.[2]

When a member wishes to prevent the consideration of an original main motion that has just been made, he or she rises, even if another has the floor, and says, "Mr./Madame Chair, I object to its consideration." The chair immediately puts the question, "The consideration of the question has been objected to. Will the assembly consider it? [or, Shall the question be considered?]" If decided in the negative by a two-thirds vote, the whole matter is dismissed for that session. Otherwise, the discussion continues as if this objection had never been made. Any question that is dismissed may be introduced at any succeeding session.

The ***Object*** of this motion is not to cut off debate (for which other motions are provided) but to enable the assembly to avoid altogether any question that it may deem irrelevant, unprofitable, or contentious. If the chair considers the question entirely outside the objects of the society, he or she should rule it out of order. This decision may be appealed.

Objection to the consideration of a question must not be confused with objecting where unanimous consent or a majority vote is required. Thus, in the case of the minority of a committee desiring to submit their views, a single member saying "I object" prevents it, unless the assembly by a majority vote grants them permission.

24. Division of a Question, and Consideration by Paragraph or by Seriatim. ***Division of a Question.***[3] The motion to divide a question can be applied only to main motions and to amendments. It takes precedence only over the motion to postpone indefinitely. It yields to all privileged, incidental, and subsidiary motions except to amend and to postpone indefinitely. It may be amended but can have no other subsidiary motion applied to it. It is undebatable. It may be made at any time when the question to be divided or the motion to postpone indefinitely is immediately pending, even after the previous question has been ordered. It is preferable to divide the question when it is first introduced. When divided, each resolution or proposition is considered and voted on separately, just as if it had been offered alone. The motion to adopt, which was pending when the question was divided, applies to all the parts into which the question has been divided and therefore should not be repeated. A formal vote on dividing the question is generally dispensed with. It is usually arranged by general consent. If this cannot be done, a formal motion to divide is necessary, specifying the exact method of division.

When a motion relating to a certain subject contains several parts, each of which is capable of standing as a complete proposition if the others are removed, it can be divided into two or more propositions to be considered and voted on as distinct questions. The assembly adopts a motion to divide the question in a specified manner. The motion must clearly state how the question is to be divided. Any member may propose a different division. These different propositions or amendments should be treated as filling blanks **[33]** and should be voted on in the order in which they are made. If they suggest different numbers of questions, the largest number is voted on first. If a resolution includes several distinct propositions, but is so written that they cannot be separated without its being rewritten, the question cannot be divided. The division must not require the secretary to do more than mechanically separate the resolution into the required parts, prefixing to each part the words ***Resolved, That,*** or ***Ordered, That,*** dropping conjunctions when necessary, and replacing pronouns by the nouns for which they stand wherever the division makes it necessary. When the question is divided, each separate question must be a proper one for the assembly to act upon if none of the others is adopted. Thus, a motion to ***commit with instructions*** is indivisible, because, if divided and the motion to commit should fail, the other motion to instruct the committee would be absurd because there would be no committee to instruct. The motion to ***strike out certain words and insert others*** is strictly one, indivisible proposition.

When a series of independent resolutions relating to different subjects is included in one motion, it must be divided on the request of a single member. This request may be made while another has the floor. However, regardless of how complicated a *single* proposition may be, no member has a right to insist upon its division. If it is capable of division, the solution is to move that it be divided. If it cannot be divided, the member should move to strike out the objectionable parts. A motion to strike out a name in a resolution brings the assembly to a vote on that name just as well as would a division of the question.

A series of resolutions proposed as a substitute for another series cannot be divided. However, a motion can be made to strike out any of the resolutions before the vote is taken on the substitution. After they have been substituted it is too late to strike out any of them. When a committee reports a number of amendments to a resolution referred to it, one vote may be taken on adopting or agreeing to all the amendments. However, if a single member requests votes on one or more of the amendments, these must be considered separately. The others may all be voted on together.

Consideration by Paragraph or Seriatim. Elaborate propositions, such as a series of resolutions on one subject or a set of by-laws where the parts are intimately connected, should not be divided. Division would make much more difficult the perfection of the different paragraphs or by-laws by amendments. If the paragraphs are adopted separately and amendments to succeeding paragraphs make it necessary to amend a preceding one, it can be done only by first reconsidering the vote on the preceding paragraph. The difficulty is even greater in the case of by-laws, because each by-law goes into effect as soon as adopted and its amendment is controlled by any by-law or rule that may have been adopted on the subject.

When the paragraphs are voted on separately, no vote should be taken on the whole. In all such cases the proper course is to consider the proposition by paragraph, section, or resolution, or ***seriatim***, as it is often called. The chair should always adopt this course when the question consists of several paragraphs or resolutions. If the chair thinks the assembly wishes to act immediately on them as a whole, he or she asks if they shall be taken up by paragraph and the matter is settled informally. Should the chair neglect to take up the proposition by paragraph or seriatim, anyone may move that the proposition be so considered.

This method of procedure in acting upon a complicated report, such as a set of by-laws or a series of resolutions that cannot well be divided, is as follows (the word ***paragraph*** is used to designate the natural subdivisions, whether they are paragraphs, sections, articles, or resolutions). The member submitting the report obtains the floor and says that the committee submits the following report or that the committee recommends the adoption of the following resolutions. He or she reads the report or resolutions and moves their adoption. Should the member neglect to move their adoption, the chair should call for such a motion or may assume the motion and state the question accordingly. The chair, or the secretary, or the member who reported it, as the chair decides is in the best interest of the assembly, then reads the first paragraph, which is explained by the reporting member, after which the chair asks, "Are there any amendments to this paragraph?" The paragraph is then open to debate and amendment. When no further amendments are proposed to this paragraph, the chair says, "There being no further amendments to this paragraph the next will be read." In this manner each paragraph is read in succession, explained if necessary, debated, and amended, the paragraphs being amended but not adopted. After all the paragraphs have been amended, the chair declares the entire by-law, paper, or resolution open to amendment. Additional paragraphs may then be inserted and any paragraph may be further amended. When the paper is satisfactorily amended, the preamble, if any, is treated the same way, and then a single vote is taken on the adoption of the entire paper, report, or series of resolutions. The previous question can be ordered on a resolution, a series of resolutions, or on a set of by-laws before the preamble has been considered. This does not apply to the preamble, unless expressly so stated, because the preamble cannot be considered until after debate has ceased on the resolutions or by-laws. It is unnecessary to amend the numbers of the sections, paragraphs, etc. It is the secretary's duty to make all such corrections where amendments make changes necessary.

25. Division of the Assembly, and Motions Relating to Methods of Voting, or to Closing and Reopening the Polls. ***A Division of the Assembly*[4]** may be called for without obtaining the floor at any time after the question has been put, even after the vote has been announced and another has the floor, provided the vote was taken *viva voce* or by show of hands. Division must be called for before another motion has been made. This call, or motion, is made by saying, "I call for a division ," or "I doubt the vote," or simply by calling out, "Division." It does not require a second. It cannot be debated, amended, or have any other subsidiary motion applied to it. As soon as a division is called for, the chair proceeds to take the vote again by having the affirmative rise, and then, when they are seated, having the negative rise. While any member has the right to insist upon a rising vote or a division when there is any doubt that a vote is the true expression of the assembly's will, the chair should guard against obstructive abuse of this privilege by members who constantly demand a division when there is a full vote and the outcome is clear. A majority vote is required to order the vote to be counted, to be taken by yeas and nays (roll call), or by ballot. These motions are incidental to the question that is pending or has just been pending and cannot be debated. When different methods are suggested they are usually treated not as amendments, but like filling blanks, the vote being taken first on the method of voting that takes the most time. The method of taking a vote is generally agreed upon without the formality of a vote.

When the vote is taken by ballot during a meeting of the assembly, as soon as the chair thinks all have voted who wish to, he or she inquires if all have voted. If there is no response, the chair declares the polls closed, and the tellers proceed to count the vote. A formal motion made to close the polls should not be recognized until all have presumably voted. It then requires a two-thirds vote, like motions to close debate or nominations. If members enter afterwards, the polls can be reopened by a majority vote. None of these motions are debatable.

26. Motions Relating to Methods of Making, or to Closing or to Reopening Nominations. If the by-laws or rules designate no method of making nominations, and the assembly has adopted no order on the subject, anyone can make a motion prescribing the method of nomination for an office to be filled. If the election is pending, this motion is incidental to it; if the election is not pending, it is an incidental main motion. It is undebatable. When it is an incidental motion it can have no subsidiary motion applied to it except to amend. It yields to privileged motions. The motion may provide that nominations be made by the chair, from the floor (*open nominations*), by a nominating committee to be appointed, or by ballot or mail. [See *Nominations and Elections*, **66.**]

Closing and Reopening Nominations. When nominations have been made from the floor or by a committee, the chair should ask if there are any further nominations before proceeding to an election. If there are none, the chair declares the nominations closed. In large assemblies a motion is usually made to close nominations. This motion is only in order after a reasonable time has elapsed. It is a main motion, incidental to the nominations and elections. It cannot be debated. It can be amended as to the time, but can have no other subsidiary motions applied to it. It yields to privileged motions and requires a two-thirds vote because it deprives members of one of their rights.

27. Requests Growing out of Business Pending or that has just been Pending. During the meetings of a deliberative assembly there are occasions when members wish to obtain information or to do or to have done things that require their making a request. Among these the following are treated separately below: *(**a**) Parliamentary Inquiry; (**b**) Request for Information; (**c**) Leave to Withdraw a Motion; (**d**) To Read Papers; (**e**) To be Excused from a Duty; (**f**) Request for any other Privilege.*

(a) Parliamentary Inquiry. A parliamentary inquiry that relates to a question requiring immediate attention may be made while another has the floor. It may even interrupt a speech, but should interrupt a speaker no more than is necessary to respond to the inquirer. It yields to privileged motions that are in order when the inquiry is made. It cannot be debated or amended or have any other subsidiary motion applied to it. The inquirer does not obtain the floor, but rises and says, "Mr./Madame Chair, I rise to a parliamentary inquiry." The chair asks the member to state his or her question. If the chair deems it pertinent, he or she answers it. If an inquiry is made when another has the floor, the chair may defer answering it until after the speaker has concluded.

While it is not the chair's duty to answer questions of parliamentary law in general, the chair should respond to a member's request for information that is pertinent to the pending business and may be necessary to enable the member to make a suitable motion or to raise a point of order. The chair should know parliamentary law. Many of the members do not. For instance, when a member wishes to have the assembly act immediately on a subject that is in the hands of a committee and the member does not know how to accomplish this, his or her recourse is a parliamentary inquiry.

(b) Request for Information. A request for information relating to the pending business is treated just as a parliamentary inquiry, and has the same privileges. The inquirer rises and says, "Mr./Madame Chair, I rise for information," or, "I rise to a point of information." The chair then directs the member to state the point on which he or she desires information. The procedure continues as in the case of a parliamentary inquiry. If the information is desired of the speaker instead of the chair, the inquirer upon rising says, "Mr./Madame Chair, I should like to ask the lady/gentleman a question." The chair inquires if the speaker is willing to be interrupted. If he or she consents, the chair directs the inquirer to proceed. The inquirer then asks the question through the chair, thus, "Mr./Madame Chair, I should like to ask the lady/gentleman," etc. The reply is made in the same way. It is out of order for members to address one another in the assembly. While each speaker addresses the chair, the chair remains silent during the conversation. If the speaker consents to the interruption, the time consumed is taken out of his or her time.

(c) Leave to Withdraw a Motion.[5] A request for leave to withdraw a motion or a motion to grant such leave may be made at any time before voting on the question has begun, even when the motion has been amended. It requires no second. It may be made while incidental or subsidiary motions are pending. These motions cease to be before the assembly when the question to which they are incidental or subsidiary is withdrawn. It yields to privileged motions. It cannot be amended or have any other subsidiary motion applied to it. It is undebatable. When it is too late to renew it, the motion to reconsider can only be withdrawn with unanimous consent. When a motion is withdrawn, the effect is just as if it had never been made. Until the chair states a motion, the mover may withdraw or modify it without asking anyone's consent. If the mover modifies it, the seconder may withdraw his or her second. After the question has been stated it is in the possession of the assembly and the mover can neither withdraw nor modify it without the consent of the assembly. When the mover requests permission to modify or withdraw his or her motion, the chair asks if there is any objection. If there is none the chair announces that the motion is withdrawn or is modified. If anyone objects, the chair puts the question on granting the request or a motion may be made to grant it. In case the mover of a main motion wishes to accept an amendment that has been offered, without obtaining the floor, he or she says, "Mr./Madame Chair, I accept the amendment." If no objection is made, the chair announces the question as amended. If anyone objects, the chair states the question on the amendment, as it can be accepted only by general consent. A request for leave to do anything is treated the same as a motion to grant the leave. This request must be made by the maker of the motion it is proposed to modify. The motion to grant the leave is made by another member. It requires no second because it is favored by the one making the request.

(d) To Read Papers. If any member objects, a member has no right to read or have the clerk read from any paper or book as a part of his speech without the assembly's permission. The request or motion to grant such permission yields to privileged motions. It cannot be debated, amended, or have any other subsidiary motion applied to it. It is customary, however, to allow members to read printed extracts as parts of their speeches as long as they do not abuse the privilege.

When papers are laid before the assembly, every member has a right to have them read once. If there is a debate or amendment a member has the right to have them read again before he or she can be compelled to vote on them. Whenever a member asks for the reading of any such paper, evidently for information and not for delay, the chair should direct it to be tion and not for delay, the chair should direct it to be read if no one objects. But a member does not have the right to have anything read (except as stated above) without permission of the assembly. A member who is absent when the paper under consideration was read, even though absent on duty, cannot insist on its being read again. The convenience of the assembly is more important than that of a single member.

(e) To be Excused from a Duty. A member, elected to office, appointed to a committee, or assigned any other duty, who is unable or unwilling to perform the duty or fill the office, should decline it immediately if present. If absent, the member should upon learning of it at once notify the secretary or the president orally or in writing that he or she cannot accept the duty. Most organizations cannot compel their members to accept office or perform any duties not required by the by-laws. A member who does not immediately decline accepts the office and is under obligation to perform the duty until there has been a reasonable opportunity to accept his or her resignation. The secretary, for instance, cannot relieve himself or herself from the responsibility of the office by resigning. This responsibility does not end until his or her resignation is accepted, or at least until a reasonable time has passed. It is seldom good policy to refuse a resignation. Just as a member has no right to continue to hold an office the duties of which he or she cannot or will not perform, so a society has no right to force an office on an unwilling member. When a member declines an office, a motion is only necessary when the by-laws of the society make the performance of such duties obligatory upon members. If the member is present at the election, the vacancy is filled as if no one had been elected. If the member is not present at the election, when the chair announces his or her refusal to take the office, as it is a question of privilege relating to the organization of the society, the election to fill the vacancy may take place immediately unless notice is required, or other provision for filling vacancies is provided by the by-laws. In the case of a resignation, the chair may at once state the question on accepting it, or a motion to that effect may be made. In either case it is debatable and may have any subsidiary motion applied to it. It yields to privileged and incidental motions.

(f) Request for any other Privilege. A member must rise and address the chair to make any request, stating at once why he or she rises. When the floor is assigned to another, the member should make his or her request only when certain that the urgency of the case justifies it. As a rule, all such questions are settled informally or by general consent. If objection is made, a vote is taken. An explanation may be requested or given, but there is no debate. Such requests should be treated with fairness, but in a manner that interrupts the proceedings as briefly as possible.

Article V: Subsidiary Motions

28. LAY ON THE TABLE
29. THE PREVIOUS QUESTION
30. LIMIT OR EXTEND LIMITS OF DEBATE
31. POSTPONE DEFINITELY, OR TO A CERTAIN TIME
32. COMMIT OR REFER, OR RECOMMIT
33. AMEND
34. POSTPONE INDEFINITELY

28. Lay on the Table. This motion takes precedence over all other subsidiary **[12]** motions and over any incidental **[13]** questions that are pending when it is made. It yields to privileged **[14]** motions and to motions that are incidental to itself. It is undebatable and cannot have any subsidiary motion applied to it. It can be applied to: ***(a)*** *any main* **[11]** *motion;* ***(b)*** *to any question of privilege or order of the day after it is before the assembly for consideration;* ***(c)*** *to an appeal that does not adhere to the main question,* so that the action on the latter would not be affected by the reversal of the chair's decision; and ***(d)*** *to the motion to reconsider when immediately pending,* in which case the question to be reconsidered also goes to the table.

No motion that has another motion adhering to it

can be laid on the table by itself. When laid on the table it carries with it everything that adheres to it. When it is taken from the table **[35]** everything is in the same condition (as much as possible) as when the motion was laid on the table. However, if the motion is not taken up until the next session, the effect of the previous question is exhausted. When the ordering of the previous question or some other means closes debate, the questions still before the assembly may be laid on the table until the last vote is taken under the order. For example, if the previous question is ordered on a series of questions when a resolution and an amendment and a motion to commit are pending, and the vote is taken and lost on the motion to commit, it is in order to lay on the table the resolution that carries with it the adhering amendment.

This motion can be applied only to a question actually pending. It is not in order to lay on the table a *class* of questions such as the orders of the day, unfinished business, or committee reports. These are not pending questions, because only one main motion can be pending at a time.

The correct method to accomplish the desired object, which is clearly to reach a special subject or class of business, is to suspend the rules by a two-thirds vote and take up the desired question or class of business. Sometimes when it is desired to pass over the next order or class of business, that business is ***passed*** by general consent. As soon as the business for which it was ***passed*** is disposed of, it is taken up again. By general consent, the business to come before the assembly may be considered in any order the assembly wishes.

When a motion to lay on the table has been made and lost, or when a question laid on the table is taken from the table, the assembly clearly wishes to consider the question immediately. For this reason, a renewal made the same day of the motion to lay that question on the table is out of order until there has been material progress in business or debate, or unless an unforeseen and urgent matter requires immediate attention. Motions relating to adjournment or recess, made and lost, are not business that justifies the renewal of the motion to lay on the table. It might be justified after the vote on an important amendment, or on the motion to commit.

If the motion to lay on the table is adopted, the question may be taken from the table as soon as the interrupting business has been disposed of and while no question is pending, and business of this class, or new or unfinished business, is in order.

The *Form* of this motion is "I move to lay the question on the table," or "that the question lie on the table." It cannot be qualified in any way. If it is qualified as "to lay the question on the table until 2 P.M.", the chair should state it properly as a motion to postpone until 2 P.M. This is a debatable question. It is not a motion to lay on the table.

The ***Object***[1] of this motion is to enable the assembly to attend to more urgent business, in laying aside the pending question in a way that permits the assembly to resume consideration of it as easily as if it were a new question and in preference to new questions competing with it for consideration. It is in the assembly's interest that this object should be reached instantly by a majority vote. This motion must therefore either apply to or take precedence over every debatable motion whatever its rank. It is undebatable, and requires only a majority vote, regardless of the fact that the question is suppressed if not taken from the table. These dangerous privileges are given to no other motion whose adoption would result in final action on a main motion. It can be tempting to make improper use of them and lay questions on the table for the purpose of instantly suppressing them by a majority vote instead of using the previous question, the legitimate motion to bring the assembly to an immediate vote. The fundamental principles of parliamentary law require a two-thirds vote for every motion that suppresses a main question for the session without free debate. The motion to lay on the table, being undebatable, requiring only a majority vote, and having the highest rank of all subsidiary motions, is in direct conflict with these principles when used to suppress a question. If habitually used in this way, it should, like any other motion to suppress without debate, require a two-thirds vote.

The minority has no remedy for the unfair use of this motion, but its abuse can be contained. The person who introduces a resolution is sometimes cut off from speaking by the motion to lay the question on the table being made as soon as the chair states the question, or even before. In such cases the introducer of the resolution should always claim the floor, to which he or she is entitled. Members often make this motion so hastily that they neglect to address the chair and obtain the floor. In such instances one of the minority should quickly address the chair. If not given the floor, this member can make the point of order that he or she was first to address the chair, and that the other member, not having the floor, was not entitled to make a motion [3].

Because motions laid on the table are merely temporarily laid aside, the majority should remember that the minority may all stay to the moment of final adjournment and then be in the majority and take up and pass the resolutions laid on the table. They may also take the question from the table at the next meeting in societies having regular meetings as frequently as quarterly. The safer and fairer method is to object to the consideration of the question if it is so objectionable that it is not desired even to allow its introducer to speak on it. Alternatively, if there has been debate so it cannot be objected to, the previous question can be moved. If adopted, this immediately brings the assembly to a vote. These are legitimate motions for determining immediately whether the assembly wishes discussion of a subject. Because they require a two-thirds vote, no one has a right to object to their being adopted.

The ***Effect*** of the adoption of this motion is to place on the table (i.e., in charge of the secretary) the pending question and everything adhering to it. When an amendment is pending to a motion to refer a resolution to a committee, and the question is laid on the table, all these questions go together to the table. They all come up together when taken from the table. An amendment proposed to anything already adopted is a main motion. When it is laid on the table, it does not carry with it the thing proposed to be amended. A question of privilege may be laid on the table without carrying with it the question it interrupted.

In legislative bodies and all other assemblies that do not have regular sessions as often as quarterly, questions laid on the table usually remain there for that entire session, but they can be taken up before the session closes. In deliberative bodies with regular sessions as frequently as quarterly, the sessions are usually very short and questions laid on the table remain there until the close of the next regular session, if not taken up earlier; just as in the same assemblies a question can be postponed to the next session, and the effect of the motion to reconsider, if not called up, does not terminate until the close of the next session. The reasons for any of these rules apply with nearly equal force to the others. While a question is on the table no motion on the same subject is in order that would in any way affect the question that is on the table. The question must first be taken from the table. The new motion can then be proposed as a substitute, or another motion can be made.

29. The Previous Question[2] is simply a motion to close debate and proceed to vote on the immediately pending question and any other pending questions on which it has been ordered. It takes precedence over all subsidiary **[12]** motions except to lay on the table **[28]**, to which it yields. It yields to privileged **[14]** and incidental **[13]** motions. It is undebatable and cannot be amended or have any other subsidiary motion applied to it. It may be qualified in order to apply to a series of pending questions or to a consecutive part of a series beginning with the immediately pending question. The effect of an amendment can be obtained by calling for the previous question on a different set of pending questions. This set must be consecutive and include the immediately pending question. In this case the vote is first taken on the motion that orders the previous question on the largest number of questions. The previous question can be applied to any debatable or amendable motion or motions. If unqualified, it applies only to the immediately pending motion. It requires a two-thirds vote for its adoption.

After the previous question has been ordered, up to the time of taking the last vote under it, the questions that have not been voted on may be laid on the table, but can have no other subsidiary motions applied to them. An appeal made after the previous question has been demanded or ordered, and before its exhaustion, is undebatable. The previous question may be reconsidered before any vote has been taken under it, but not after its partial execution. Because no one would vote to reconsider the vote ordering the previous question who was not opposed to it, if the motion to reconsider prevails it will be impossible to secure a two-thirds vote for the previous question. Therefore, if it is voted to reconsider the previous question, it is considered as rejecting that question and placing the business as it was before the previous question was moved. If a vote taken under the previous question is reconsidered before the previous question is exhausted, there can be no debate or amendment of the proposition. However, if the reconsideration occurs after the previous question is exhausted, then both the motion to reconsider and the question to be reconsidered are divested of the previous question and are debatable. If lost, the previous question may be renewed after progress in debate sufficient to make it a new question.

The *Form* of this motion is "I move [or demand, or call for] the previous question on [here specify the motions on which it is desired to be ordered]." Because the previous question cannot be debated or amended, it must be voted on immediately. The form of putting the question[3] is "The previous question is moved [or demanded, or called for] on [specify the motions on which the previous question is demanded]. As many as are in favor of ordering the previous question on [repeat the motions] will rise." When they are seated the chair continues: "Those opposed will rise. There being two-thirds in favor of the motion, the affirmative has it and the previous question is ordered on [repeat the motions upon which it is ordered]. The question is [or recurs] on [state the immediately pending question]. As many as are in favor," etc. If the previous question is ordered, the chair immediately proceeds to put to vote the questions on which it was ordered until all the votes are taken, or there is an affirmative vote on postponing definitely or indefinitely, or committing, either of which exhausts the previous question. If there is the slightest doubt as to the vote, the chair should retake it immediately. If less than two-thirds vote in the affirmative, the chair announces the vote thus: "There not being two-thirds in favor of the motion, the negative has it and the motion is lost. The question is on," etc., the chair stating the question on the immediately pending question, which is again open to debate and amendment, just as if the previous question had not been demanded. The question may be put in this form: "The previous question has been moved on the motion to commit and its amendment. As many as are in favor of now putting the question on the motion to commit and its amendment will rise; those opposed will rise. There being two-thirds in favor of the motion, the debate is closed on the motion to commit and its amendment, and the question is on the amendment," etc. While this form is allowable, it is better to conform to the regular parliamentary form as given above.

The *Object* of the previous question is to bring the assembly immediately to a vote on the immediately pending question and on other pending questions that are specified in the demand. It is the correct motion to use for this purpose, whether the object is to adopt or to kill the proposition on which it is ordered without further debate or motions to amend.

The *Effect*[4] of ordering the previous question is to close debate immediately, to prevent the moving of amendments or any other subsidiary motions except to lay on the table, and to bring the assembly immediately to a vote on the immediately pending question and any other pending questions that are specified in the demand. If the previous question is ordered on more than one question, its effect extends to those questions and is not exhausted until they are voted on or disposed of (discussed below under exhaustion of the previous question). If the demand for the previous question is voted down, discussion continues as if the motion had not been made. The effect of the previous question does not extend beyond the session in which it is adopted. Should any of the questions upon which it is ordered come before the assembly at a future session they are divested of the previous question and are open to debate and amendment.

The previous question is ***Exhausted*** during the session as follows: *(1) When the previous question is unqualified, its effect ends when the vote is taken on the immediately pending question. (2) If the previous question is ordered on more than one of the pending questions, its effect is not exhausted until all questions upon which it has been ordered have been voted on, or the effect of those that have been voted on has been to commit the main question, or to postpone it definitely or indefinitely.*

The previous question is *not* exhausted when questions on which it has been ordered, but have not been voted on, are laid on the table. When these are taken from the table during the same session, they are still under the previous question and cannot be debated or amended or have any other subsidiary motion applied to them.

30. Limit or Extend Limits of Debate. Like the demand for the previous question, motions or orders to limit or extend the limits of debate take precedence over all debatable motions. They can be applied to any debatable motion or series of motions. If not otherwise specified, they only apply to the immediately pending question. When it is voted to limit the debate, the order applies to all incidental and subsidiary motions and to the motion to reconsider, if subsequently made, as long as the order is in force. An order extending the limits of debate applies to the immediately pending motion and to others only as specified. These orders are undebatable and require a two-thirds vote for their adoption. They may be amended, but can have no other subsidiary motion applied to them. They yield to privileged **[14]** and incidental **[13]** motions, and to motions to lay on the table **[28]** and for the previous question **[29]**. They may be made only when the immediately pending question is debatable. When one of them is pending, another one that does not conflict with it may be moved as an amendment. After one of these motions has been adopted it is in order to move another one of them, if it does not conflict with the one in force. The motion to limit or extend the limits of debate may be reconsidered even when the order has been partially executed. If lost, it may be renewed after there has been sufficient progress in debate to make it a new question.

After an order is adopted to close debate at a certain hour, or to limit it to a certain time, the motions to postpone and to commit cannot be moved until the vote adopting the order has been reconsidered. However, the pending question may be laid on the table. If it is not taken from the table until after the hour appointed for closing the debate and taking the vote, no debate or motion to amend is allowed. The chair should immediately put the question (demand the vote). After the adoption of an order limiting the number or length of the speeches, or extending these limits, it is in order to move any of the other subsidiary **[12]** motions on the pending question. An order modifying the limits of debate on a question is in force only during the session in which it is adopted. If the question in any way goes over to the next session it is divested of this order and is open to debate according to the regular rules.

The various *Forms* of this motion are as follows: *(1) To fix the hour for closing debate and putting the question*: "I move that debate close and the question be put on the resolution at 9 P.M." (2) *To limit the length of the debate*: "I move that debate on the pending amendment be limited to twenty minutes." *(3) To reduce or increase the number and length of speeches*: "I move that debate on the pending resolution and its amendments be limited to one speech of five minutes from each member"; "I move that Ms. A's time be extended ten minutes"; or "I move that Ms. A and Mr. B [the leaders on the two sides] be allowed twenty minutes each, to be divided between their two speeches at their pleasure, and that other members be limited to one speech of two minutes each, and that the question be put at 9 P.M."

31. Postpone Definitely or to a Certain Time.[5] This

takes precedence over the motions to commit, to amend, and to postpone indefinitely. It yields to all privileged **[14]** and incidental **[13]** motions, and to the motions to lay on the table **[28]**, for the previous question **[29]**, and to limit or extend the limits of debate **[30]**. The motion to postpone can be debated, but debate should go into the merits of the main question only as necessary to enable the assembly to determine the propriety of the postponement. The motion to postpone can be amended as to the time. It can also be amended by making the postponed question a special order. The previous question and the motions limiting or extending the limits of debate may be applied to it. It cannot be laid on the table alone. When the motion to postpone is pending, the main question must be laid on the table. This carries with it the motion to postpone. It cannot be committed or postponed indefinitely. It can be reconsidered. A two-thirds vote is required to make a question a special order.

The time to which a question is postponed must fall within the session or the next session.[6] If it is desired to postpone a question to the next regular session, the time for the adjournment of that meeting must be fixed before a question may be postponed to it. Some societies have frequent meetings for social or other purposes at which some business may be transacted, and hold a monthly or quarterly meeting especially for business. In such societies these rules apply particularly to the regular business meetings. Questions may be postponed from the previous regular business meeting or from any of the intervening meetings.

No motion to postpone definitely nor any amendment to it is in order that has the effect of an indefinite postponement that defeats a measure (for instance, to postpone until tomorrow a motion to accept an invitation for tonight). When the motion to postpone indefinitely is in order, the chair treats it at his or her discretion, but it cannot be recognized as a motion to postpone definitely. It is not in order to postpone a class of business such as committee reports. Each report may be postponed when announced or called for. The rules may be suspended by a two-thirds vote to enable the assembly to take up a question. A matter that the by-laws require to be attended to at a specified time or meeting—the election of officers, for instance—cannot be postponed in advance to another time or meeting. At the specified time or meeting the assembly may postpone the matter to an adjourned meeting. This is sometimes advisable, for instance when an annual meeting for the election of officers occurs when only a few members can attend. After an order of the day or a question of privilege is before the assembly for action, its further consideration may be postponed or any other subsidiary motion may be applied to it. When a question has been postponed to a certain time, it becomes an order of the day for that time and cannot be taken up before that time except by a reconsideration or by suspending the rules for that purpose. This requires a two-thirds vote. [See *Orders of the Day,* **20,** for the treatment of questions that have been postponed definitely.]

The Form of this motion depends on the objective: ***(1)*** *Simply to postpone the question to the next meeting when it will have precedence over new business, the form is* "I move to postpone the question [or, that the question be postponed] to the next meeting." It then becomes a general order for that meeting. ***(2)*** *To specify an hour when the question will be taken up as soon as the question then pending, if there is any, is disposed of, the form is* "I move that the question be postponed to 3 P.M." ***(3)*** *To postpone the question until after a certain event, when it shall immediately come up, the form is* "I move to postpone the question until after the speech." ***(4)*** *To insure that the question will not be crowded out by other matters, the following words should be added to the motion to postpone as given in the first two cases above:* "and be made a special order." Or the motion may be made thus: "I move that the question be postponed and made a special order for the next meeting [or, for 3 P.M. tomorrow]." The motion in this form requires a two-thirds vote, because it suspends the rules that may interfere with its consideration at the time specified [See *Orders of the Day,* **20.**] ***(5)*** *To postpone a question to an adjourned meeting and devote the entire time, if necessary, to its consideration,* as in the case of revising by-laws, after providing for the adjourned meeting the motion should be made in this form: "I move that the question be postponed and made the special order for next Tuesday evening." Alternatively, a question may be postponed and made the special order for the next regular meeting.

The ***Effect*** of postponing a question is to make an order of the day for the time to which it was postponed. If it is not then disposed of, it becomes unfinished business. Postponing a question to a certain hour only becomes a special order when the motion specifies it. The motion to postpone definitely may be amended by a majority vote to make the amended motion one that makes the question a special order. If this is done, the amended motion requires a two-thirds vote. [See *Orders of the Day,* **20.**]

32. Commit or Refer, or Recommit. (Except where stated otherwise, all the rules in regard to this motion apply equally to the motions *to go into Committee of the Whole, to Consider Informally,* and *to Recommit.*) This motion takes precedence over the motions to amend and to postpone indefinitely. It yields to all the other subsidiary **[12]** motions and to all privileged **[14]** and incidental **[13]** motions. It cannot be applied to any subsidiary motion, nor can it be laid on the table or postponed except in connection with the main question. The previous question, motions to limit or extend the limits of debate, and motions to amend may be applied to it without affecting the main question. It is debatable but only as to the propriety of committing the main question.[7] If the motion to postpone indefinitely is pending when a question is referred to a committee, it is lost and is not referred to the committee. Pending amendments go with the main motion to the committee. The motion to commit may be reconsidered. However, after the committee has begun consideration of the question referred to it, it is too late to move to reconsider the vote to commit. The committee may, however, then be discharged as shown below.

The *form* of the motion to commit (i.e., to refer to a committee) may vary from the simple form "that the question be referred to a committee" to the complete form of referring the question "to a committee of five to be appointed by the chair, with instructions to report resolutions properly covering the case at the next regular business meeting." If the motion is made in the complete form, the details may be changed by amendments, usually treated not as ordinary amendments but as in filling blanks **[33]**.

Three methods are followed in completing the details when the motion is made in the simple form of merely referring the pending question to a committee. From these one is chosen that best suits the case: ***(1)*** *The simple, or skeleton, motion may be completed* *by moving amendments or making suggestions for adding the required details as stated above.* **(2)** *The chair on his or her own initiative may call for suggestions to complete the motion.* The chair first asks to which committee the question shall be referred, and then continues in the order shown below. ***(3)*** *The motion in its simplest form may be put to vote at once by its enemies' ordering the previous question.* When the motion to commit is almost certain to be lost, this is sometimes done to save the time that would be uselessly spent in completing the details. If the motion to commit is adopted, which is improbable in this circumstance, the details are completed before any new business (except privileged matters) can be taken up. These details are taken up in the order given below, the chair calling for the several items much as if he or she were completing the motion before it was voted on.

In completing the motion simply to refer to a committee, the first question the chair asks is "To what committee shall the question be referred?" If different committees are suggested, the suggestions are not treated as amendments of those previously offered. They are voted on in the following order until one receives a majority vote: **(a)** *committee of the whole;* **(b)** *as if in committee of the whole;* **(c)** *consider informally;* **(d)** *standing committee,* in the order in which they are proposed; **(e)** *special (select) committee,* largest number voted on first.

If the question has already been before a standing

or special committee the motion becomes the motion to recommit. The committees would be voted on in the above order except the old committee would precede other standing and select committees. In suggesting or moving that the committee be a special one, the word ***special*** is not generally used, the motion being made to refer the question to a committee of five, or any other number that makes it a special committee—i.e., not a standing committee. If any committee except a special one is decided upon, the chair should then put the question on referring the question to that committee. Any member may interrupt the chair and move to add instructions. The chair may suggest them, or instructions may be given after the vote has been taken on committing the question. Instructions may be given to the committee by a majority vote at any time before it submits its report, even at another session.

If the committee is to be a special one, in addition to the number of members it must be decided how they are to be appointed. If different methods are suggested or moved, they are voted on in the following order: ***(a)*** *ballot;* ***(b)*** *nominations from the floor* (or *open nominations*); ***(c)*** *nominations by the chair;* or ***(d)*** *appointment by the chair* (the method that should usually be adopted in very large assemblies). When the method of appointment is decided, the completed motion to commit is put to vote. Instructions as stated above may be added before the vote is taken on the motion to commit, or they may be given afterwards. If the motion to commit is adopted, no new business (except privileged matters) can intervene until the appointment of the committee by the method prescribed. However, the chair, when appointing the committee, is allowed time to make his or her selections. These selections must be announced to the assembly.

If objection is made, a member can make only one nomination from the floor. In a large assembly the nominating member rises and addresses the chair without waiting to be recognized, saying, "I nominate Ms. A." In small assemblies members often remain seated when making nominations to committees. The chair repeats each name as he or she hears it. If no more than the prescribed number are suggested, the chair puts the question on the members named constituting the committee. If more names than the prescribed number are suggested, the chair puts the question on each name in succession, beginning with the first named, until enough are chosen to fill the committee. The negative must be put as well as the affirmative, a majority vote being required for each member of the committee. If the committee is nominated by the chair, he or she states the question thus: "The question is 'Shall these members constitute the committee?'" It is now in order to move to strike out any of the names. If such a motion is adopted the chair replaces them with other names. No vote is taken when the chair appoints the committee, but he or she must announce the names of the committee to the assembly. The committee cannot act until this announcement is made. Sometimes it is desired to permit the chair to appoint a committee after adjournment. This must be authorized by a vote. The power to appoint a committee carries with it the power to appoint its chair and to fill any vacancy that may arise in the committee. The resignation of a member of a committee should be addressed to the appointing power.

The *Forms* of this motion are as follows: (a) "To refer the question to a committee"; (b) "To recommit the resolution"; (c) "That the subject be referred to a committee of three to be appointed by the chair, and that it report by resolution at the next meeting"; (d) "That it be referred to a committe with power"; (e) "That the assembly does now resolve itself into [or, go into] committee of the whole, to take under consideration," etc., specifying the subject **[55]**; (f) "That the resolution be considered as if in committee of the whole" **[56]**; and (g) "That the resolution be considered informally" **[57]**.

The *Object* of the motion to refer to a standing or special committee is usually to enable a question to be more carefully investigated and put into better shape for the assembly to consider than can be done in the assembly itself. Where an assembly is large and has a great volume of business, it is safer to have every main question go to a committee before final action on it is taken. A special committee to investigate and report upon a subject should consist of representative members on both sides of the question, so that both parties in the assembly may have confidence in the report or reports when there is disagreement and a minority report is submitted. With care in selecting committees in ordinary assemblies, debates upon delicate and troublesome questions can be mostly confined to the committees. It is not required to appoint on the committee the member who makes the motion to refer. However, this is the usual and courteous thing to do when the member is particularly interested and informed on the subject. If the appointing power does not designate a committee chair, the member first named acts as such unless the committee chooses to elect one. It is consequently important that the first named should be an efficient person, especially in a committee for action.

Sometimes a question is referred to a committee with full power to act in the case. When the duty assigned to it has been performed, it should report what it has done. The committee ceases to exist after this report has been made. When the assembly has decided a question and appoints a committee to take certain action (such as a committee of arrangements for holding a public meeting), the committee should be small and its entire membership in favor of the action to be taken. A member appointed to such a committee who does not support the proposed action should say so and ask to be excused. Such a committee is sometimes given power to add to its number.

The object of ***going into committee of the whole,*** or considering a question ***as if in committee of the whole,*** or ***informally,*** is to enable the assembly to discuss a question with perfect freedom. The number of speeches is not limited. The latter is the simplest method and is best adapted to ordinary societies that are not large. [See Sections **55–57**.]

If any form of the motion to commit is made in reference to a question not pending, it becomes a main motion. A motion to go into committee of the whole on a question not pending, to appoint a committee upon a subject not pending, or to appoint a committee to take certain action is thus a main motion.

Discharge a Committee. When a committee makes its final report and the assembly receives it, the committee ceases to exist. No motion needs to be made to this effect. If the assembly wishes to take a question out of the hands of a committee, and it is too late to reconsider the vote on the committal, it is necessary to ***discharge the committee from further consideration*** of the resolution or other matter referred to it. As long as the matter is in the hands of the committee, the assembly cannot consider anything that practically involves the same question. If the committee has not yet taken up the question referred to it, the proper motion (on the day or the day after it was referred) is to reconsider the vote to commit. This requires only a majority vote. If the motion to reconsider cannot be made, a motion to discharge the committee should be made. If adopted, this practically rescinds action taken. It therefore requires a two-thirds vote, or a vote of the majority of the membership. If previous notice of the motion has been given, it requires only a majority vote. When a committee is discharged, the chair returns to the secretary all papers that have been entrusted to him or her. A motion is required to bring the matter referred before the assembly. This motion may be combined with the motion to discharge, thus: "I move that the committee to whom was referred the resolution on immigration be discharged, and that the resolution be now taken up for consideration [or, be considered at some other specified time]."[8]

33. Amend. This takes precedence over the motion to postpone indefinitely. It yields to all other subsidiary **[12]** motions and to all privileged **[14]** and incidental **[13]** motions, except the motion to divide the question. It can be applied to all motions except those in the *List of Motions that Cannot be Amended* [see below in this section]. It can be amended itself, but this ***amendment of an amendment*** (an amendment of the second degree) cannot be amended. The previous question and motions to limit or extend the limits of debate may be applied to an amendment, or only to an amendment of an amendment. In such cases they do not affect the main question, unless so specified. An amendment is debatable in all cases except when the motion to be amended is undebatable. An amendment of a pending question requires only a majority vote for its adoption, even when the question to be amended requires a two-thirds vote. An amendment of a previously adopted constitution, by-laws, rules of order, or order of business requires a two-thirds vote; but an amendment of that amendment requires only a majority vote. When a motion or resolution is under consideration only one amendment of the first degree is permitted at a time, and one amendment of that amendment (i.e., an amendment of the second degree) is allowed also. An amendment of the third degree would be too complicated and is not in order.[9] Instead of making it, a member may say that if the amendment of the amendment is voted down, he or she will offer an alternative to the amendment of the amendment. While there can be only one amendment of each degree pending at the same time, any number of them may be offered in succession. An amendment must be germane[10] to the subject to be amended. An amendment to an amendment must be germane to the latter.

An amendment may be in any of the following **Forms**: ***(a) to insert*** or ***add*** (i.e., ***place at the end***); ***(b) to strike out; (c) to strike out and insert,*** or to ***substitute,*** as it is called, when an entire paragraph or resolution is struck out and another is inserted.

The third form combines the first two. It cannot be divided, though, as shown below, for the purposes of amendment the two motions are treated separately, the words to be struck out being first amended and then the words to be inserted. No amendment is in order whose effect is to convert one of these forms into another.

The motion to amend is made in this form: "I move to amend the resolution by inserting the word 'very' before the word 'good'"; or it may be reduced to a form as simple as this: "I move to insert 'very' before 'good.'" The motion to insert should always specify the word before or after which the insertion is to be made. The motion to strike out should also locate the word when it occurs more than once. When the chair states the question on the amendment he or she should repeat the motion in detail so that all may understand what modification is proposed. Unless the effect of the amendment is obvious, the chair in putting the question should show clearly the effect of its adoption, even if this requires the reading of the entire resolution, and then the words to be inserted, or struck out, or struck out and inserted, and finally the resolution as it will stand if the amendment is adopted. The chair then says, "As many as are in favor of the amendment [or of striking out, etc., or of inserting, etc.] say aye; those opposed, say no." The ayes have it, the amendment is adopted, and the question is on the resolution as amended, which is, "Resolved, That," etc., reading the resolution as amended. If the vote is taken by show of hands or by rising, the question is put and the vote announced thus: "As many as are in favor of the amendment will rise [or will raise the right hand]; those opposed will rise [or will manifest it in the same way]. The affirmative has it and the amendment is adopted. The question is on the resolution," etc. The instant the amendment is voted on, whether it is adopted or lost, the chair should announce the result of the vote and state the question that is then before the assembly.

To ***Insert*** or ***Add*** words. When a motion to ***insert*** [or ***add***] certain words is made, the words to be inserted should be perfected by amendments proposed by their friends before the vote is taken on inserting them. After words have been inserted they can be changed or struck out only by a motion to strike out the paragraph or whatever portion of it that makes the question entirely different from the prior version in which the particular words were inserted. Such a motion (to strike out the paragraph or a portion of it) can be combined with the motion to insert other words. The principle involved is this: When the assembly has voted that certain words shall form a part of a resolution, it is not in order to make another motion that involves exactly the same question as the one it has decided. The only way to bring it up again is to move to reconsider **[36]** the vote by which the words were inserted. If the motion to insert is lost, it does not preclude any other motion to insert these words together with other words, or in place of other words, provided the new motion presents an essentially new question to the assembly.

To ***Strike out Words.*** The motion to strike out certain words can be applied only to consecutive words, though as the result of amendments the words may be separated when the final vote is taken. Separate motions must be made to strike out separated words. Still better, a motion may be made to strike out the entire clause or sentence containing the words to be struck out and to insert the desired new clause or sentence. The motion to strike out certain words may be amended only by striking out words from the amendment. The effect of the adoption of both motions is the retention in the resolution of the words struck out of the amendment. If the motion to strike out certain words is adopted, the same words cannot be inserted again unless the place or the wording is so changed that a new proposition is made. If the motion to strike out fails,[11] it does not preclude a motion to strike out the same words and insert other words, or to strike out a part of the words, or to strike out a part and insert other words, or to strike out these words with others, or to do this and insert other words. In each of these cases the new question is materially different from the old one. [For striking out all or a part of something that has been previously adopted, see *Rescind,* etc., **37**]. To ***Strike Out*** and ***Insert Words*** is a combination of the two preceding motions, and is indivisible.[11] For purposes of amendment it is resolved into its constituent elements. The words to be struck out are first amended, after which are amended the words to be inserted. After their amendment the question is put on the motion to strike out and insert. If it is adopted, the inserted words cannot be struck out nor can the words struck out be inserted unless the words or place are so changed as to make the question a new one as described above. If the motion is lost, it does not preclude either of the single motions to strike out or insert the same words nor another motion to strike out and insert, provided there is any material change in either the words to be struck out or the words to be inserted so that the questions are not practically identical. When it is desired to strike out or modify separated words, a motion may be made to strike out as much of the resolution as necessary to include all the words to be struck out or changed, and to insert the desired revision including these words. If the words are inserted in the place previously occupied by the words struck out, they may differ materially from the latter, provided they are germane to it. If the words are to be inserted at a different place, then they must not differ materially from those struck out, as it must be in the nature of a transfer. The combined motion to strike out words in one place and to insert different words in another place is not in order. Either the place or the words must be substantially the same. If there are several changes to be made, it is usually better to rewrite the paragraph and offer it as a substitute as shown below.

Amendments Affecting an Entire Paragraph. A motion to ***insert*** [or ***add***] or to ***strike out*** a paragraph, or to ***substitute*** one paragraph for another, is an amendment of the first degree. It therefore cannot be made when an amendment is pending. The friends of the paragraph to be inserted or struck out should put it in the best possible shape by amending it before it is voted on. After a paragraph has been inserted it cannot be amended except by adding to it. It cannot be struck out except in connection with other paragraphs in a way that makes the question essentially new. If the paragraph is struck out, it cannot be inserted afterward unless it is so changed in wording or place as to present an essentially new question. If the motion to insert or to strike out a paragraph is lost, it does not preclude any other motion except one that presents essentially the same question that the assembly has already decided, as shown above in the case of amending words of a paragraph. Thus, when a motion to insert a paragraph has been lost, it is in order to move or insert a part of the paragraph or the entire paragraph if materially altered. So, though the assembly has refused to strike out a paragraph, it is in order to strike out a part of the paragraph or otherwise to amend it. It is safer, however, for its friends to make it as nearly perfect as possible before the vote is taken on striking it out, with an aim to defeat that motion.

After the chair states it, the motion to ***substitute*** one paragraph for another (this combines the two preceding motions) is resolved into its two elements for the purpose of amendment. The chair first entertains amendments only to the paragraph to be struck out, these amendments being of the second degree. After it is perfected by its friends, the chair asks if there are any amendments proposed to the paragraph to be inserted. When both paragraphs have been perfected by amendments the question is put on substituting one paragraph for the other. Even though the paragraph constitutes the entire resolution and the motion to substitute is carried, a vote on adopting the resolution must be taken afterward, because it has only been voted to substitute one paragraph for another. A paragraph that has been substituted for another can only be amended afterward by adding to it, like any other paragraph that has been inserted. The paragraph that has been replaced cannot be again inserted unless so modified as to constitute a new question, as with any paragraph that has been struck out. If the motion to substitute is lost, the assembly has only decided that that particular paragraph shall not replace the one specified. It may be willing that it replace some other paragraph, or that it be inserted, or that the paragraph retained in the resolution be further amended or even struck out. But no amendment is in order that presents to the assembly essentially the same question that it has already decided.

To speak of ***substituting*** one word or part of a paragraph for another is incorrect parliamentary language. This term is applied to nothing less than a paragraph. When a question is considered by section, it is in order to move a substitute for the pending section. A substitute for the entire resolution or report cannot be moved until all sections have been considered and the chair announces that the entire paper is open to amendment. When a resolution with amendments of the first and second degree pending is referred to a committee, they may report it back with a recommended substitute for the resolution, even though two amendments are pending. In this case the chair first states the question on the amendments that were pending when the resolution was committed. When they are disposed of, he or she states the question on the substitute recommended by the committee and proceeds, as in the case of any other substitute motion.

An amendment is improper and out of order that: ***(a)*** *is not germane to the question to be amended;* ***(b)*** *merely makes the affirmative of the amended question equivalent to the negative of the original question;* ***(c)*** *is identical with a question previously decided by the assembly during that session;* ***(d)*** *changes one form of amendment to another form;* ***(e)*** *substitutes one form of motion for another form;* ***(f)*** *strikes out the* *word* **Resolved** *from a resolution;* ***(g)*** *strikes out or inserts words that would leave no rational proposition before the assembly;* or ***(h)*** *is frivolous or absurd.*

An amendment of an amendment must be germane to (relate to) the subject of the amendment as well as to the main motion. No independent new question can be introduced under cover of an amendment. An amendment in conflict with the spirit of the original motion and yet still relevant to it is in order.

Illustrations: A resolution of censure may be amended by striking out the word **"censure"** and inserting the word **"thanks."** Both words relate to opinions of conduct. Refusing to censure is not the same as expressing thanks.

A resolution to purchase books cannot be amended by striking out the word **"books"** and inserting the word **"buildings."** Suppose a pending resolution directs the treasurer to buy a desk for the secretary. An amendment is offered to add the words **"and pay the expenses of the delegates to the State Convention."** This amendment is not germane to the resolution. Paying the expenses of the delegates does not relate to buying a desk for the secretary. Therefore this is out of order. However, an amendment offered to insert the words **"and buy a permanent record book"** after the word **"desk"** would be in order, because both articles enable the secretary to perform his or her duties.

A pending resolution commending certain things can be amended by adding other things that are similar or relate to them. Suppose a resolution commending A and B for heroism is pending. If the acts of heroism were not connected, amendments are in order adding other names for other acts of heroism. However, if the commendation is for an act of heroism in which A and B were joined, then no names can be added to the resolution unless the parties were connected with A and B in that act.

Suppose the following resolution is pending: "Resolved, That the Secretary be instructed to notify our representative in Congress that we do approve his course in regard to the tariff." A motion to amend by inserting "not" after the word "be" would be out of order because an affirmative vote on "not instructing" is identical in effect with a negative vote on "instructing." But the motion to insert the word "not" after "do" is in order because an affirmative vote on disapproving of a certain course is not the same as a negative vote on a resolution of approval. The latter may only indicate an unwillingness to express an opinion on the subject.

A resolution is pending and a member makes the motion "*I move to strike out the words* 'pine benches' *and insert the words* 'oak chairs.'" This is an amendment of the first degree. No other amendment of that degree is in order until it is acted upon. All the words in italics are necessary for this form of motion, and are not subject to amendment. The only amendments in order are those that change the words **"pine benches"** to **"oak chairs"**—that is, first those to be struck out, and when they are perfected, then those to be inserted. Suppose the motion to **"strike out 'pine'"** is pending, and it is moved to amend by adding **"and insert 'oak.'"** This motion is out of order, because it changes one form of amendment to another form.

It is not in order to move to strike out the word ***adopt*** in a motion and insert the word ***reject,*** because ***adopt*** is a formal word necessary to show the kind of motion made. Practically, however, the same result may be attained by moving to postpone indefinitely—that is, to reject, the main question.

The chair should never rule an amendment out of order unless he or she is certain that it is so. When in doubt the chair should admit the amendment or submit the question of its being in order to the assembly [described in **21**].

Every original main motion may be amended. All others may be amended, except those contained in the following list. ***Motions That Cannot Be Amended:*** *To adjourn* (except when it is qualified, or when made in an assembly with no provision for a future meeting) **[17]**; *Call for the orders of the day* **[20]**; *Question of order, and appeal* **[21]**; *To object to consideration of a question* **[23]**; *Call for a division of the assembly* **[25]**;

To grant leave to withdraw a motion [**27**]; *To grant leave to speak after indecorum* [**21**]; *A request of any kind* [**27**]; *To take up a question out of its proper order* [**22**]; *To suspend the rules* [**22**]; *To lay on the table* [**28**]; *To take from the table* [**35**]; *To reconsider* [**36**]; *The previous question* [**29**]; *To postpone indefinitely* [**34**]; *To amend an amendment* [**33**]; *To fill a blank* [**33**]; *A nomination* [**66**].

A motion to adopt a resolution or a by-law may be amended by adding "and that it be printed and that members be supplied with copies," or "that they go into effect at the close of this annual meeting," or anything of a similar kind.

Under each of the privileged, incidental, and subsidiary motions, whether the motion may be amended or not is stated. The way in which it may be amended is explained when necessary.

An amendment to anything already adopted is not a subsidiary motion. The matter to be amended is not pending and is therefore not affected by anything done with the amendment, provided it is not adopted. Such an amendment is a main motion subject to amendments of the first and second degrees.

The motion to strike out an entire resolution that has been adopted is usually called to *Rescind* [**37**].

[For motions to amend a by-law, etc., See **68**, *Amendments of Constitutions, By-laws*, etc.]

Minutes are usually amended (corrected informally, the chair directing the correction to be made when suggested). If objection is made, a formal vote is necessary for the amendment. The minutes may be corrected whenever the error is noticed, regardless of the time that has elapsed. However, after their adoption, when it is too late to reconsider the vote, they require a two-thirds vote for their amendment unless previous notice of the proposed amendment has been given. Only a majority vote is then required for its adoption, just as with the motion to rescind **[37]**. This is necessary for the protection of the records that otherwise would be subject to risk of being tampered with by temporary majorities.

The numbers prefixed to paragraphs, articles, etc., are only marginal indications and should be corrected by the secretary, if necessary, without any motion to amend. [For amending a long paper, such as a series of resolutions, or a set of by-laws, which should be considered and amended by paragraph, see **24.**]

Filling Blanks.[12] Propositions for filling blanks are treated somewhat differently from other amendments. Any number of members, without a second, propose different names or numbers for filling the blanks. No member can propose more than one name or number for each place unless by general consent. These are treated not as amendments (one of another), but as independent propositions to be voted on successively. If the blank is to be filled with a name, the chair repeats the names as they are proposed so all may hear them and then takes a vote on each name, beginning with the first proposed, until one receives a majority vote. If the blank is to be filled with several names and no more names are suggested than required, the names may be inserted without a vote. If more names than required are suggested, a vote is taken on each, beginning with the first, until enough to fill the blank have received a majority vote. If the number of names is not specified, a vote is taken on each name suggested, and all that receive a majority vote are inserted.

If the blank is to be filled with a number or a date, then the largest sum, the longest time, or the most distant date is put first unless it is clear to the chair that the reverse order is necessary to enable the first vote to be taken on the proposition that is least likely to be adopted.

Illustrations: Suppose a committee is to be instructed to purchase a building for a blank amount. The voting on filling the blank should begin with the largest sum proposed. If that is lost, all who voted for it and some others would favor the next largest sum, thus resulting in a larger vote. This sequence is continued until the largest sum that a majority will approve is reached. If the voting began with the smallest sum, everyone would be willing to pay that amount. It might be adopted and thus cut off voting on the other propositions, whereas a majority would prefer authorizing the committee to spend a larger amount. On the other hand, suppose the committee is to be authorized to sell a building for a blank amount; here it is evident that there would be more in favor of a large sum than of a small one. The will of the assembly is best determined if the voting begins with the smallest sum proposed. Members willing to sell for that amount and some others will be willing to sell for the next larger sum. The smallest sum for which the majority is willing to sell will be gradually reached.

It is sometimes convenient to create a blank. For example, a pending resolution requests the proper authorities to prohibit the erection of commercial buildings north of A street. Amendments to strike out A and insert B, and to strike out B and insert C, are made. The debate develops the fact that several other streets have their advocates. The best course is for the chair to state that if there is no objection the motion will be treated as having a blank for the name of the street, and that A, B, and C are proposed for filling the blank. In this way other names can be suggested. These can be voted on successively, beginning with the one that makes the prohibited area the largest, and continuing down until one is reached that wins a majority in its favor. If objection is made to leaving a blank for the name, the chair may put the question without waiting for a motion, or anyone may move as an incidental motion that a blank be created for the name of the street. This motion is undebatable. It cannot be amended, but it may be moved to fill the blank by ballot or in any other way.

The blanks in a resolution should usually be filled before voting on the resolution. Sometimes a large majority is opposed to the resolution and the previous question is ordered without waiting for the blanks to be filled. This stops debate and further amendment, and brings the assembly at once to a vote on the resolution. In this case the resolution is usually rejected. If it is adopted, the blanks in the skeleton resolution must be filled before any other than privileged business is in order.

The method adopted in filling blanks sometimes has a great advantage over ordinary amendment. In amending, the last one proposed is the first one voted on, whereas in filling blanks, the first one proposed (or nominated) is voted on first, except when the nature of the case makes another order preferable. That order is then adopted as explained above.

Nominations are treated like filling blanks. Any number may be pending at the same time, not as amendments of each other, but as independent propositions to be voted on in the order in which they were made until one receives a majority vote **[66.]**

34. Postpone Indefinitely. This is simply a motion to reject the main question. It only takes precedence over the main motion to which it is applied. It yields to all privileged **[14]**, incidental **[13]**, and other subsidiary [12] motions. It cannot be amended or have any other subsidiary motion applied to it except the previous question and motions limiting or extending the limits of debate. It is debatable and opens the main question to debate. It can be applied only to main questions. This includes questions of privilege and orders of the day after they are before the assembly for consideration. An affirmative vote on it may be reconsidered, but not a negative vote. If lost it cannot be renewed. If a main motion is referred to a committee while to postpone indefinitely is pending, the latter motion is ignored and does not go to the committee.

The ***Object*** of this motion is not to postpone but to reject the main motion without incurring the risk of a direct vote on it. It is only made by the enemies of the main motion when they doubt that they are in the majority.

The ***Effect*** of making this motion enables members who have exhausted their right of debate on the main question to speak again, because the question technically before the assembly is different, although there is no difference caused by changing the question from adopting to rejecting the measure as far as the subject of discussion is concerned. The merits of the main question are open to debate in both cases. If adopted, it suppresses the main motion for that session unless the vote is reconsidered. Because this motion does not suppress the debate on the main question, its only use is to give the opponents of the pending measure a chance of killing the main motion without risking its adoption in case of failure. If they carry the indefinite postponement, the main question is suppressed for the session. If they fail, they still have a vote on the main question, and, having learned their strength by the vote taken, they can judge the advisability of continuing the struggle.

Article VI: Some Main and Unclassified Motions

35. TAKE FROM THE TABLE
36. RECONSIDER
37. RESCIND, REPEAL, OR ANNUL
38. RENEWAL OF A MOTION
39. RATIFY
40. DILATORY, ABSURD, OR FRIVOLOUS MOTIONS
41. CALL OF THE HOUSE

35. Take from the Table takes precedence over no pending question. When no question is actually pending and new or unfinished business is in order, it does have preference over main motions when it is applied to a motion that has been laid on the table during the session. It is also valid at the next session of societies that have regular business meetings as frequently as quarterly. It yields to privileged **[14]** and incidental **[13]** motions, but not to subsidiary **[12]** motions. It is undebatable. No subsidiary motion can be applied to it. It is only in order after some business has been transacted since the question was laid on the table. If lost, the motion to take from the table cannot be reconsidered, but it can be renewed after some business has been transacted. If carried, the question can be again laid on the table after progress in debate or business.

In ordinary deliberative assemblies, a question should be laid on the table only temporarily, with the expectation that its consideration will be resumed after the interrupting question is disposed of, or at a more convenient time.[1] After the question is disposed of that was introduced when the first question was laid on the table, any member may move to take the first question from the table. When a member rises to make this motion, if the chair recognizes someone else as having first risen, the member should immediately say that he or she rises to move to take a question from the table. The chair then assigns him or her the floor if the other member has risen to make a main motion. If the chair states the new main motion before the member claims the floor, his or her motion is not in order until the new question is disposed of.

When taken up, the question with everything adhering to it is before the assembly exactly as it was when laid on the table. If a resolution has amendments and a motion to commit when it is laid on the table, when it is taken from the table the question is first on the motion to commit. If a motion to postpone to a certain time is pending when the question is laid on the table, and it is taken from the table after that time, then the motion to postpone is ignored when the question is taken up.

If the question is taken up on the day it was laid on the table, members who have exhausted their right of debate cannot again speak on the question. If taken up on another day, no notice is taken of previous speeches. The previous question is not exhausted if the question upon which it was ordered is taken from the table at the same session, even though it is on another day.

36. Reconsider.[2] This motion is peculiar in that the making of the motion has a higher rank than its consideration. For a certain time it prevents anything being done as the result of the vote it proposes to reconsider. It can be made only on the day the vote to be reconsidered was taken or on the next day (a legal holiday or a recess is not counted as a day). It must be made by a member who voted with the prevailing side. Any member may second it. It can be made while any other question is pending, even if another member has the floor, or after it has been voted to adjourn if the chair has not announced adjournment. It may be made after the previous question has been ordered. In this case, the motion to reconsider and the motion to be reconsidered are both undebatable.

While the making of the motion to reconsider has such high privilege, its consideration has only the rank of the motion to be reconsidered, though it does take preference over any new motion of equal rank, as shown below. Even when the general orders are being carried out, the reconsideration of a vote that either temporarily or permanently disposes of a main question may be called up if no question is pending. The motion to reconsider cannot be amended, postponed indefinitely, or committed. If the reconsideration is laid on the table or postponed definitely, the question to be reconsidered and all adhering questions go with it.[3] The previous question and the motions extending the limits of debate may be applied to it when it is debatable. It is undebatable only when the motion to be reconsidered is undebatable. When debatable it opens to debate the merits of a question to be reconsidered. It cannot be withdrawn after it is too late to renew the motion. If the motion to reconsider is lost it can only be repeated by general consent. No question can be twice reconsidered unless it was materially amended after its first reconsideration. A reconsideration requires only a majority vote, regardless of the vote necessary to adopt the motion reconsidered.

The motion to reconsider ***cannot be applied***: ***(a)*** *to a vote on a motion that may be renewed within a reasonable time;* ***(b)*** *when practically the same result may be obtained by some other parliamentary motion;* ***(c)*** *when the vote has been partially executed* (except in the case of the motion to limit debate) *or something has been done as the result of the vote that the assembly cannot undo;* ***(d)*** *to an affirmative vote in the nature of a contract, when the other party to the contract has been notified of the vote;* or ***(e)*** *to a vote on the motion to reconsider.*

In accordance with these principles, votes on the following motions ***cannot be reconsidered:*** ***(a)*** *Adjourn;* ***(b)*** *Take a Recess;* ***(c)*** *Lay on the Table;* ***(d)*** *Take from the Table;* ***(e)*** *Suspend the Rules or Order of Business;* ***(f)*** and *Reconsider.*

Affirmative votes on the following cannot be reconsidered: ***(a)*** *Proceed to the Orders of the Day;* ***(b)*** *Adopt,* or after they are adopted, to *Amend,* or *Repeal,* or *Rescind* the *Constitution, By-laws,* or *Rules of Order,* or any other rules whose amendment require previous notice; ***(c)*** *Elect to membership or office* if the member or officer is present and does not decline, or if absent and has learned of his election in the usual way and has not declined; ***(d)*** to *Reopen Nominations.*

A negative vote on the motion to *Postpone Indefinitely* cannot be reconsidered, because the same question essentially comes up again when the vote is taken on the main question.

After a committee has taken up the matter referred to it, it is too late to reconsider the vote committing it, though the committee may be discharged. But after debate has proceeded under an order limiting or extending the limits of debate, the vote making that order may be reconsidered because the debate may develop facts that make it desirable to return to the regular rules of debate. The minutes (or record of proceedings) may be corrected at any time without reconsidering the vote approving them.

If the main question is pending and a member moves to reconsider the vote on any subsidiary **[12]**, incidental **[13]**, or privileged **[14]** motion, the chair states the question on the reconsideration the moment the motion to be reconsidered is in order, provided it is then made for the first time. For example, when the motions ***(a)** to commit,* ***(b)** for the previous question,* and ***(c)** to lay on the table,* are pending if it is moved to reconsider a negative vote on postponing to a certain time, the chair first takes the vote on laying on the table. If that is lost, the vote is taken on the previous question and then on reconsidering the vote on the postponement. If the latter is adopted, a vote is taken on the postponement. If this is lost, then a vote is taken on the motion to commit. When the motion to lay on the table is carried, the same method of procedure is followed as when the question is taken from the table;

i.e., the question is first on ordering the previous question, next on reconsidering the vote on the postponement, etc.

If the reconsideration of an amendment of the first degree is moved while another amendment of the same degree is pending, the pending amendment is first disposed of and then the chair announces the question on the reconsideration of the amendment. When the reconsideration of an amendment to an immediately pending question is moved, the chair immediately announces the question on the reconsideration.

If the reconsideration is moved when another subject is before the assembly, it cannot interrupt the pending business, but, as soon as that has been disposed of, if called up it has preference over all other main motions and general orders. In such cases the chair states the question on the reconsideration when it is called up.

If the motion to reconsider is made when the reconsideration could be called up if it had been previously made, the chair immediately states the question on the reconsideration, unless the mover adds to his motion the words **"and have it entered on the minutes,"** as explained below.

If, after the vote has been taken on the adoption of the main motion, it is desired to reconsider the vote on an amendment, the vote on the main question must also be reconsidered. One motion should be made to cover both votes. The same principle applies in the case of an amendment to an amendment, whether the vote has been taken on the resolution, or only on the amendment of the first degree.

When the motion covers the reconsideration of two or three votes, the debate is limited to the question that was first voted on. Thus, if the motion is to reconsider the votes on a resolution and amendments of the first and second degree, the debate is limited to the amendment of the second degree and recognizes the mover of the reconsideration as entitled to the floor. The question is now in exactly the same condition it was in just previous to taking the original vote on that amendment.

The *Forms* of making this motion are as follows: (a) "I move to reconsider the vote on the resolution relating to a banquet." (b) "I move to reconsider the vote on the amendment to strike out 'Wednesday' and insert 'Thursday.'" This form is used when the resolution is still pending. (c) "I move to reconsider the votes on the resolution relating to a banquet and on the amendment to strike out 'Wednesday' and insert 'Thursday.'" This form is used when the vote has been taken on the resolution, and reconsideration of the vote on an amendment is desired.

When the motion to reconsider is made, the chair states the question, if it can then be considered, and proceeds as with any other question. If it cannot be considered at that time, the chair says, "Ms. A moves to reconsider the vote on . . . The secretary will make a note of it." The chair then continues with the pending business.

The reconsideration, after being moved, is brought before the assembly for action as explained above. If it is ***called up*** by a member, after obtaining the floor he or she simply says, "I call up the motion to reconsider the vote on . . . " This call requires no second or vote.

If the call is in order, as previously explained, the chair says, "The motion to reconsider the vote [or votes] on . . . is called up. The question is, 'Will the assembly reconsider the vote [or votes] on . . . ? Are you ready for the question?'"

If the reconsideration is one that the chair states the question on as soon as it can be considered (as when it is moved to reconsider an amendment while another amendment is pending), as soon as the proper time arrives, the chair states the question on the reconsideration just as if the motion to reconsider were made at this time.

When the debate, if there is any, is finished, the chair *puts the question* thus: "As many as are in favor of reconsidering the vote on the resolution relating to a banquet, say aye; those opposed say no. The ayes have it and the vote on the resolution is reconsidered. The question is now on the resolution, which is," etc. The question may also be put thus: "The question is, Will the assembly reconsider the votes on the resolution relating to a banquet, and on the amendment to strike out 'Wednesday' and insert 'Thursday?' As many as are in favor of the reconsideration say aye; those opposed say no. The ayes have it and the votes on the resolution and the amendment are reconsidered. The question is now on the amendment, which is," etc.

If the motion to reconsider is adopted, business is in exactly the same condition it was in before taking the vote or the votes that have been reconsidered. The chair instantly states the question on the immediately pending question, which is then open to debate and amendment as before.

The ***Effect of Making*** this motion is to suspend all action that the original motion would have required until the reconsideration is acted upon. If the motion to reconsider is not called up, its effect ends with the session[4] **[63]**, except in an assembly having regular meetings as often as quarterly. In this case, if not called up, its effect does not end until the close of the next regular session. As long as its effect lasts, anyone at an adjourned, special, or regular meeting may ***call up*** the motion to reconsider and have it acted upon. It is unusual, however, for anyone other than the mover to call it up on the day it is made if the session lasts beyond that day and there is no need of prompt action.

The ***Effect of the Adoption*** of this motion is to place before the assembly the original question in the exact position it occupied before it was voted upon. Consequently, after the reconsideration is adopted, no member can debate the question reconsidered who had on that day exhausted his or her right of debate on that question. The member's only recourse is to discuss the question while the motion to reconsider is before the assembly. When the question is not reconsidered until a later day than that on which the vote to be reconsidered was taken, it is open to free debate regardless of previous speeches. When a vote taken under the operation of the previous question is reconsidered, the question is divested of the previous question and is open to debate and amendment, provided the previous question had been exhausted by votes taken on all the questions covered by it before the motion to reconsider was made.

In *standing* and *special* committees a vote may be reconsidered regardless of the time elapsed since the vote was taken, provided that: ***(a)*** *the motion is made by one who did not vote with the losing side,* ***(b)*** *all members who voted with the prevailing side are present,* or ***(c)*** *have received due notice that the reconsideration would be moved at this meeting.* A vote cannot be reconsidered in committee of the whole.

Reconsider and Have Entered on the Minutes.[5] The motion to reconsider, as explained above, provides means for correcting (at least on the day on which they occur) errors due to hasty action. By using the same motion and having it entered on the minutes so that it cannot be called up until another day, a means is provided to prevent a temporary majority from taking action that the majority of the society opposes. This is needed in large societies with frequent meetings and small quorums, where attendance is often less than 10 percent of the membership. It protects the members of such societies from injudicious action by temporary majorities, without requiring previous notice of main motions and amendments. To accomplish this form of the motion, however, ***Reconsider and Have Entered on the Minutes*** must be allowed to apply to a vote finally disposing of a main motion, regardless of the fact that the motion to reconsider has already been made. Otherwise it would be useless, because it would generally be blocked by the motion to reconsider in its simple form, which would be voted down. This motion then could not be made. Because this form of the motion is designed for use only when the meeting is an unrepresentative one, this fact should be very clear.

Some members of the temporary minority should vote with the temporary majority on adopting or postponing indefinitely a main motion of importance when they think the action is contrary to the wishes of the great majority of the society. One of them should then move "to reconsider the vote on the resolution [or motion] and have it [or request that it be] entered on the minutes." This has the effect of suspending all action required by the vote it is proposed to reconsider, as previously explained, and thus gives time to notify absent members of the proposed action. If no member of the temporary minority voted with the majority, and it is too late for anyone to change his or her vote in order to move to reconsider, then someone should give notice of a motion to rescind the objectionable vote at the next meeting. This may be done by a majority vote at the meeting following the one at which this notice is given.

Should a minority make an improper use of this form of the motion to reconsider by applying it to a vote that requires action before the next regular business meeting, the remedy is immediately to vote that when the assembly adjourns it adjourns to meet on another day, appointing a suitable day when the reconsideration could be called up and disposed of. The mere taking of this motion would probably cause the withdrawal of the motion to reconsider, as it would defeat the object of that motion if the majority of the society is in favor of the motion to be reconsidered. If the motion to reconsider is withdrawn, of course the other would be.

This form of the motion ***to reconsider and have entered on the minutes*** differs from the simple form to reconsider in the following respects: ***(a)*** *It can be made only on the day the vote to be reconsidered is taken.* If a meeting is held on the next day, the simple form of the motion to reconsider, made then, accomplishes the object of this motion by bringing the question before the assembly on a different day from the one when the vote was taken. ***(b)*** *It outranks the simple form of the motion to reconsider, and may be made even* *after the vote has been taken on the motion to reconsider, provided the result of the vote has not been announced.* If made after the simple form of the motion to reconsider, it supersedes the latter, which is thereafter ignored. ***(c)*** *It can be applied only to votes that finally dispose of the main question.* These are an affirmative or negative vote on adopting, and an affirmative vote on postponing a main question indefinitely. It may also be applied to a negative vote on the consideration of a question that has been objected to, provided the session extends beyond that day. ***(d)*** *In an assembly not having regular business meetings as often as quarterly, it cannot be moved at the last business meeting of a session.* ***(e)*** *It cannot be called up on the day it is made, except when it is moved on the last day of a session of an assembly not having regular business sessions as often as quarterly, when anyone can call it up at the last business meeting of the session.* After it is called up there is no difference in the treatment of the two forms of the motion.

37. Rescind, Repeal, or Annul. To rescind is identical to the motion to amend something previously adopted, by striking out the entire by-law, rule, resolution, section, or paragraph. It is subject to all the limitations as to notice and vote that the rules apply to amendments similar to it. Any vote taken by an assembly, except those mentioned below, may be rescinded by a majority vote, provided notice of the motion has been given at the previous meeting or in the call for this meeting. Without notice, any vote may be rescinded by a two-thirds vote or by a vote of the majority of the entire membership. The notice may be given when another question is pending, but cannot interrupt a member while speaking.

The motion to rescind: **(a)** *is a main motion without any privilege, and therefore can be introduced only when there is nothing else before the assembly;* **(b)** *cannot be made if the question can be reached by calling up the motion to reconsider which has been previously made;* **(c)** *may be made by any member;* **(d)** *is debatable;* **(e)** *yields to all privileged and incidental motions; and* **(f)** *may have all of the subsidiary motions applied to it.*

The motion to rescind can be applied to votes on all main motions, including questions of privilege and orders of the day that have been acted upon, and can be applied to votes on an appeal, with the following ***exceptions:*** **(a)** *votes cannot be rescinded after something has been done as a result of that vote that the assembly cannot undo;* **(b)** *where it is in the nature of a contract and the other party is informed of the fact;* **(c)** *where a resignation has been acted upon, or someone has been elected to* (or *expelled from*) *membership or office, and was present or has been officially notified.* In the case of expulsion, the only way to reverse the action afterward is to restore the person to membership or office, which requires the same preliminary steps and vote as is required for an election.

Where it is desired not only to rescind the action but also to express very strong disapproval, legislative bodies on rare occasions have voted to rescind the objectionable resolution and ***expunge*** it from the record. This is done by crossing out the words or drawing a line around them, and writing across the the words, **"Expunged by order of the assembly,"** etc., giving the date of the order. This statement should be signed by the secretary. The words expunged must not be so blotted as to be unreadable. Otherwise it would be impossible to determine whether more was expunged than ordered. Any vote less than a majority of the total membership of an organization is certainly incompetent to expunge from the records a correct statement of what was done and recorded and the record of which was officially approved, even though a quorum is present and the vote to expunge is unanimous.

38. Renewal of a Motion. When an original main motion or an amendment has been adopted or rejected, or has been postponed indefinitely, or an objection to its consideration has been sustained, it (or anything essentially the same) can only be again brought before the assembly at the same session by a motion to reconsider or to rescind the vote. It may be reintroduced at any future session.

In assemblies with regular sessions at least as often as quarterly, a main motion can be renewed only after the close of the next regular session, if it was ***(a)*** *postponed to that next session,* **(b)** *laid on the table,* **(c)** *adopted or rejected,* or **(d)** *postponed indefinitely, and the motion to reconsider was made and not acted on at the previous session.* In these cases the question can be reached at the next session at the time to which it was postponed, by taking it from the table, or by reconsidering the vote.

In assemblies whose regular sessions are less frequent than quarterly, any motion that has not been committed or postponed to the next session may be renewed at that next session. The motions *to adjourn, to take a recess,* and *to lay on the table* may be made repeatedly, whenever there has been progress in debate or business, but the making of (or voting on) these motions is not busines that justifies the renewal of a motion. Neither a motion *to postpone indefinitely* nor an *amendment* can be renewed at the same session, but the other subsidiary motions may be renewed whenever the progress in debate or business is such as to make the question before the assembly an essentially different one.

To take from the table and *a call for the orders of the day* may be renewed after the business is disposed of that was taken up when the motion to take from the table or for the orders of the day was lost.

To postpone indefinitely cannot be renewed even

though the main motion has been amended since the indefinite postponement was previously moved.

A *point of order* cannot be raised if an identical one has been raised previously without success during the same session.

After the chair has been sustained in a ruling he or she need not entertain an appeal from a similar decision during the same session.

Minutes may be corrected regardless of the time elapsed and of the fact that the correction had been previously proposed and lost.

A subject referred to a committee and reported back at the same meeting is not a renewal, nor is a subject laid on the table and taken up at the same meeting.

The following motions, unless they have been withdrawn, ***cannot be renewed*** at the same session: ***(a)*** *to adopt* or *postpone indefinitely* an original main motion; ***(b)*** *to amend;* ***(c)*** *to reconsider,* unless the question to be reconsidered was amended materially when previously reconsidered; ***(d)*** *to object to the consideration of a question;* ***(e)*** *to fix the same time to which to adjourn;* ***(f)*** *to suspend the rules for the same purpose at the same meeting,* though it may be renewed at another meeting held the same day.

When it is evident that the *privilege of renewal* is being misused to obstruct business, the chair should protect the assembly by refusing to recognize the motions. [See *Dilatory Motions*, **40.**]

39. Ratify. This is a main motion that is used to confirm or make valid an action that requires the assembly's approval. The assembly may ratify only such actions of its officers, committees, or delegates that it has the right to authorize in advance. It cannot make valid a *viva voce* election when the by-laws require an election by ballot, nor can it ratify anything done in violation of the state laws or of its own constitution or by-laws. It may ratify emergency action taken at a meeting when no quorum was present, even if the quorum is provided for in a by-law. A motion to ratify may be amended by substituting a motion of censure, and vice versa, when the action has been taken by an officer or other representative of the assembly. It is debatable and opens the entire question to debate.

40. Dilatory, Absurd, or Frivolous Motions. The efficient functioning of deliberative assemblies requires repeated renewal of some highly privileged motions after progress in debate or the transaction of any business, and must allow a single member, by calling for a division, to have another vote taken. By taking advantage of parliamentary forms and methods, a small minority can disrupt the business of a deliberative assembly having short sessions if no provision is made to protect it. A minority of two members could constantly raise questions of order, appeal every decision of the chair, call for a division on every vote (even when nearly unanimous), move to lay motions on the table and to adjourn, and offer frivolous and absurd amendments. To deal with this problem, Congress adopted this rule: "No dilatory motion shall be entertained by the speaker."

Even without adopting any rule on this subject, every deliberative assembly has the inherent right to protect itself from disruption by members abusing parliamentary forms to prevent it from transacting the business that these very forms are designed to assist. Whenever the chair is satisfied that members are using parliamentary forms merely to obstruct business, he or she should either refuse to recognize them or rule them out of order. After the chair has been been sustained upon an appeal, he or she should not entertain another appeal from the same members while they are clearly engaged in trying by that means to obstruct business. The chair should always be courteous and fair, but should be firm in protecting the assembly from imposition, even though it be done in strict conformity with all parliamentary rules except the one rule that bars dilatory, absurd, or frivolous motions.

As an example of a frivolous or absurd motion, suppose Mr. A is to be in the city next week and a motion has been made to invite him to address the assembly at its next meeting, the meetings being weekly. The chair should rule out of order as frivolous or absurd a motion made to refer the question to a committee with instructions to report at the next regular meeting.

41. Call of the House.[6] The object of a call of the house is to compel the attendance of absent members. It is allowable only in assemblies that have the power to compel the attendance of absentees. When no quorum is present, it is usually provided that a specified small number can order a call of the house. In Congress a call of the house may be ordered by majority vote, one-fifth of the members elect present. The following rule is suitable for city councils and similar bodies that have the power to enforce attendance: ***When no quorum is present, a majority vote, one-fifth of the members elect present, may order a call of the house and compel the attendance of absent members. After the call is ordered, a motion to adjourn, or to dispense with further proceedings in the call, cannot be entertained until a quorum is present, or until the sergeant at arms[7] reports that in his opinion no quorum can be obtained on that day.***

If no quorum is present, a call of the house takes precedence over everything (even reading the minutes) except the motion to adjourn. It requires in its favor only the number specified in the rule. If a quorum is present, a call should rank with questions of privilege **[19]**, requiring a majority vote for its adoption. If rejected, it should not be renewed while a quorum is present at that meeting. After a call is ordered, until further proceedings in the call are dispensed with, no motion is in order except to adjourn and a motion relating to the call, so that a recess could not be taken by unanimous consent. An adjournment puts an end to all proceedings in the call, except that the assembly before adjournment, if a quorum is present, can order such members as are already arrested to make their excuse at an adjourned meeting.

Proceedings in a Call of the House. When the call is ordered the clerk calls the role of members alphabetically, noting the absentees. He or she then calls over again the names of the absentees, when excuses[8] can be made. The doors are then locked, and no one is permitted to leave. An order similar to the following is adopted: "Ordered, That the sergeant-at-arms take into custody, and bring to the bar of the House, such of its members as are absent without leave of the House." A warrant signed by the presiding officer and attested by the clerk, with a list of absentees attached, is then given to the sergeant-at-arms, who immediately proceeds to arrest the absentees. When the sergeant-at-arms appears with members under arrest, he or she approaches the chair (being announced by the doorkeeper in large bodies), followed by the arrested members, and makes his or her return. The chair arraigns each member separately, and asks what excuse he or she has to offer for being absent from the sittings of the assembly without its leave. The member states his or her excuse, and a motion is made that he or she be discharged from custody and admitted to his or her seat either without payment of fees or after paying the fees. Until a member has paid the assessed fees, he or she cannot vote or be recognized by the chair for any purpose.

Article VII: Debate

42. DEBATE
43. DECORUM IN DEBATE
44. CLOSING AND PREVENTING DEBATE
45. PRINCIPLES OF DEBATE AND UNDEBATABLE MOTIONS

42. Debate. The steps required before debate are explained in **1-6**. These are as follows. When no business is pending a member rises and addresses the chair. The chair then recognizes the member as having obtained the floor. The member then makes a motion that, after being seconded, is stated by the chair, who then addresses the assembly, saying, **"Are you ready for the question?"** The question is then open to debate [see **7**]. No member may speak more than twice during the same day to the same question (only once on an appeal), or longer than ten minutes at one time without leave of the assembly. The question on granting the leave is decided by a two-thirds vote without debate.[1] No member can speak a second time to a question as long as any member desires to speak who has not spoken to the question. If greater freedom is desired, the correct procedure is *to go into committee of the whole*, or *to consider it informally*. Either option requires only a majority vote. The limits of debate **[30]** may be extended. This requires a two-thirds vote. By a two-thirds vote debate may also be limited as desired.

The member whose motion brings a question before the assembly is entitled to close the debate with a speech if the member has not exhausted his or her twenty minutes, but not until anyone else wishing to speak has spoken.[2] An amendment or any other motion that is offered makes the real question before the assembly a different one. With regard to the right to debate, it is treated as a new question. When an amendment is pending the debate must be confined to the merits of the amendment, unless it is of such a nature that its decision practically decides the main question. Merely asking a question, or making a suggestion, is not considered as speaking. Though the maker of a motion can vote against it, he or she cannot speak against it. [See *Closing Debate*, **44.**]

The right of members to debate and make motions cannot be cut off by the chair's putting a question to vote with a speed that prevents the member's getting the floor after the chair has inquired if the assembly is ready for the question. Even after the chair has announced the vote, if it is found that a member has risen and addressed the chair with *reasonable promptness* after the chair asked **"Are you ready for the question?"**, the member is then entitled to the floor, and the question is in exactly the same condition it was before it was put to vote.

43. Decorum in Debate. A member is confined in debate to the question before the assembly. He or she should avoid personal comments and cannot question a member's motives, but may comdemn in strong terms the nature or consequences of a measure. It is the measure, not the man or woman, that is the subject of debate. A member can only discuss the act of the assembly that he or she is debating or against which he or she intends a motion to rescind at the conclusion of his or her remarks. In referring to another member, the member should when possible avoid using his or her name, rather referring to him or her as **"the member who spoke last"**, or otherwise describing him or her. Officers should always be referred to by their official titles.

To ask a question of the member speaking, a member should rise and without waiting for recognition say, **"Mr./Madame Chair, I should like to ask the lady/gentleman a question."** The chair then asks the speaker if he or she is willing to be interrupted, or the speaker may at once consent or decline, addressing the chair, through whom the conversation must be carried on, as members cannot directly address one another in a deliberative assembly. If the speaker consents to the question, the time consumed by the interruption comes out of his or her time.

If at any time the chair rises to state a point of order, to give information, or otherwise within his or her privilege to speak, the member speaking must take his or her seat until the chair has been heard. When called to order by the chair, the member must sit down until the question of order is decided. If his or her remarks are decided to be improper, he or she cannot proceed, if anyone objects, without the leave of the assembly expressed by a vote. No debate is allowed on this question.

The objecting member, or the secretary, should take down any disorderly words. These are then read to the offending member. If he or she denies them, the assembly decides by a vote whether they are his or her words or not. If a member cannot justify the words he or she used and will not apologize for using them, the assembly has a duty to act in the case. If the disorderly words are of a personal nature, after each party has been heard, and before the assembly proceeds to deliberate upon the case, both parties to the dispute should retire. As a general rule, no member should be present in the assembly when any matter relating to himself or herself is under debate. The member objecting to the words does not have to retire unless he or she is personally involved in the case. Disorderly words to the presiding officer, or in respect to the official acts of an officer, do not involve the officer in a way that requires him or her to retire. If any business has taken place since the member spoke, it is too late to take notice of any disorderly words he or she used.

During debate, while the chair is speaking, or the assembly is voting, no member may disturb the assembly by whispering, walking across the floor, or in any other way.

44. Closing and Preventing Debate. When the chair thinks debate is concluded, he or she asks, "Are you ready for the question?" After a reasonable pause, if no one rises to claim the floor, the chair assumes that no member wishes to speak. He or she stands and proceeds to put the question. Debate is not closed when the chair rises and puts the question. Until both the affirmative and the negative are put, a member can rise and claim the floor, and reopen the debate or make a motion, provided he or she rises with reasonable promptness after the chair asks, **"Are you ready for the question?"** If the debate is resumed the question must be put again, both the affirmative and the negative. This privilege can be abused by members who do not respond to the inquiry **"Are you ready for the**

question?", intentionally waiting until the affirmative vote is taken and then rising and reopening the debate. The chair should regard this as dilatory **[40]** and should act to protect the assembly from annoying disruption. When a vote is taken a second time, as when a division is called for, debate cannot be resumed except by general consent.

If two-thirds of the assembly wish to close the debate without allowing all the time desired by others, they can do so by ordering either the previous question or the closing of debate at a certain time. They can limit the length of the speeches and allow each member to speak only once on each question. [See **29** and **30**.] These motions require a two-thirds[3] vote, because they suspend the fundamental right of every member of a deliberative assembly to have every question fully discussed before it is finally disposed of.

A majority vote may lay the question on the table and thus temporarily suspend the debate, but it can be resumed by taking the question from the table by a majority vote when no question is before the assembly **[35]** and business of this class, unfinished business, or new business is in order. The only way to prevent discussion of a subject (even when its introducer desires to prevent it) is to object to consideration of the question **[23]** before it is debated or any subsidiary motion is stated. If the objection is sustained by a two-thirds vote, the question is thrown out for that session.

45. Principles of Debate and Undebatable Motions. All main motions are debatable. Debate is allowed or prohibited on other motions in accordance with the following principles: ***(a)** High privilege is generally incompatible with the right of debate of the privileged motion.* All highly privileged motions are therefore undebatable, except those relating to the privileges of the assembly or a member. Such questions of privilege **[19]** rarely arise. When they do, they are usually so important that they must be allowed to interrupt business. They are debatable because as a rule they cannot be intelligently acted upon without debate. The same is true of appeals from the decision of the chair that are debatable unless they relate to indecorum, to transgression of the rules of speaking, to priority of business, or are made while an undebatable question is pending. In these cases there is insufficient need of debate to justify making them an exception to the rule. An appeal under any of these circumstaces is therefore undebatable. ***(b)** Motions that have the effect of suspending a rule are not debatable.* Consequently, because they suspend the ordinary rules of debate, motions that suppress, limit, or extend the limits of debate are undebatable. ***(c)** Appeals made after the previous question has been ordered are undebatable.* It would clearly be improper to permit debate on them when the assembly by a two-thirds vote has closed debate on the pending question. So any order limiting debate on the pending question applies to questions arising while the order is in force. ***(d)*** *To Amend, or to Reconsider, an undebatable question is undebatable, whereas to amend, or to reconsider, a debatable question is debatable.* ***(e)*** *A Subsidiary motion* **[12]** *is debatable if it interferes with the right of the assembly to take up the original question at its pleasure.*

Illustrations: To ***Postpone Indefinitely*** a question places it out of the power of the assembly to take it up again during that session, except by reconsideration. Consequently, this motion can be freely debated, even involving the whole merits of the original question. To ***Commit*** a question only delays the discussion until the committee reports, when it is open to free debate, so it is only debatable as to the propriety of the commitment and as to the instructions, etc. To ***Postpone to a Certain Time*** prevents consideration of the question until the specified time, except by a reconsideration or suspension of the rules. Therefore, limited debate is allowed on the propriety of the postponement. To ***Lay on the Table*** leaves the question so that the assembly can consider it at any time that that question or that class of business is in order, and therefore to lay on the table should not be, and is not, debatable.

Because a motion is undebatable it does not follow that while it is pending the chair may not permit a question or an explanation. The distinction between debate and asking questions or making brief suggestions should be remembered. When the latter aids the assembly in transacting business, the chair should permit it before taking the vote on an undebatable question. The chair should, however, remain standing during the discussion to show that he or she has the floor, and should not allow any more delay in putting the question than he or she feels is helpful to the business.

The following lists of motions that open the main question to debate, and of those that are undebatable, are made in accordance with the above principles. ***Motions That Open the Main Question to Debate:*** *(a) Postpone Indefinitely, (b) Reconsider a Debatable Question, (c) Rescind, (d) Ratify.* **Undebatable Motions:** *(a) Fix the Time to which to Adjourn* (when a privileged question); *(b) Adjourn* (when unqualified in an assembly that has provided for future meetings); *(c) Take a Recess* (when privileged); *(d) Call for the Orders of the Day* and questions relating to priority of business; *(e) Appeal* when made while an undebatable question is pending, or when simply relating to indecorum, or transgression of the rules of speaking, or to priority of business; *(f) Suspension of the Rules; (g) Objection to the Consideration of a Question; (h) Incidental Motions,* except an *Appeal* as shown above in this list under *Appeal; (i) Lay on the Table; (j) Previous Question* **[29]** and *Motions to Close, Limit, or Extend the Limits of Debate; (k) Amend an Undebatable Motion; (l) Reconsider an Undebatable Motion.*

Article VIII: Vote

46. Voting. If the question is undebatable or debate has been closed by order of the assembly, the chair immediately states the question and puts it to vote **[9]**, only allowing time for members to rise who wish to make a motion of higher rank. If the question is debatable and no one rises to claim the floor, the chair, after stating the question, should ask, **"Are you ready for the question?"** If no one rises after a brief pause, the chair puts the question to vote. If the question is debated or motions are made, the chair should wait until the conclusion of debate, and should again ask, **"Are you ready for the question?"** The chair should give ample time for anyone to claim the floor. When no one does so, he or she should put the question to vote and announce the result.

The usual method of taking a vote is ***viva voce*** (by voice). Congressional rules require use of this method.

In small assemblies the vote is often taken by ***show of hands,*** also called ***raising the right hand.*** The other methods of voting are by ***(a)*** *rising,* ***(b)*** *ballot,* ***(c)*** *roll call,* also called *yeas and nays,* ***(d)*** *general consent,* and ***(e)*** *by mail.* In voting by any of the first three methods, the affirmative answer is *aye,* or *raise the right hand,* or *rise,* and the negative answer is *no,* or *raise the right hand,* or *rise.*

The chair should ***announce*** (or ***declare***) the vote. The chair has the right to have the vote taken again by rising. If the chair is unsure of the result, he or she can order the vote counted if necessary. The chair cannot have the vote taken by *ballot* or by *yeas and nays* (roll call) unless the rules or a vote of the assembly require it. If the *viva voce* vote does not clearly indicate the result, the chair may say, **"Those in favor of the motion will rise."** When they are seated, the chair continues, **"Those opposed will rise."** If the chair remains uncertain of the vote, he or she should say, **"Those in favor of the motion** [or **Those in the affirmative**] **will rise and stand until counted."** The chair then counts those standing, or directs the secretary to do so, and then says, **"Be seated. Those opposed** [or **Those in the negative**] **rise and stand until counted."** After both sides are counted the chair anounces the result as shown below. In a large assembly the chair may find it necessary to appoint tellers to count the vote and report the result. In small assemblies a show of hands may be substituted for a rising vote.

When the vote is taken by voice or show of hands any member has the right to require a ***division of the assembly*** **[25]** by having the affirmative rise and then the negative, so that all may see how members vote. Either before or after a decision, any member may call for or demand a count. If this is seconded, the chair must put the question on ordering a count. In organizations where it is desired to allow less than a majority vote to order a count or tellers, a special rule should be adopted specifying the necessary vote. Where no rule has been adopted a majority vote is required to order a count or to have the vote be taken by *ballot* or by *yeas and nays*.

Announcing the Vote. After a vote is taken, when the chair is sure of the result, and no division is called for (or, if so, the assembly has divided) the chair announces or declares the vote: **"The ayes have it and the resolution is adopted."** If uncertain the chair may say, **"The ayes seem to have it."** If no one then questions the vote or calls for a division, after a slight pause the chair adds, **"The ayes have it,"** etc. A vote by show of hands or by rising is announced thus: "The affirmative has it [or the motion is carried] and the question is laid on the table." When there is a count, the vote is announced thus: "There are 95 votes in the affirmative, and 99 in the negative, so the amendment is lost, and the question is now on the resolution; are you ready for the question?" In announcing a vote the chair first states whether the motion is carried or lost; second, the effect or result of the vote; and third, the immediately pending question or business if there is any. If there is none, the chair should ask, **"What is the further pleasure of the assembly?"** One of the most prolific causes of confusion in deliberative assemblies is the chair's failure to keep the assembly well informed as to what is the pending business. The habit of announcing the vote by simply saying, **"the motion is carried"** and then sitting down cannot be too strongly condemned. Many members may not know the effect of the vote. It is the chair's duty to inform the assembly of the result of the motion's being carried or lost, and what business next comes before it.

When a quorum **[64]** is present, a majority vote (i.e., a majority of the votes cast, ignoring blanks) is sufficient for the adoption of any motion that is in order, except those noted in **48**, which require a two-thirds vote. A plurality never adopts a motion or elects anyone to office, unless by virtue of a special rule previously adopted. On a tie vote the motion is lost. The chair, if a member of the assembly, may vote to make it a tie unless the vote is by ballot, but cannot vote twice, first to make a tie and then give the casting vote. In case of an appeal **[21]**, though the question is **"Shall the decision of the chair stand as the judgment of the assembly?"**, a tie vote, even though the chair's vote makes it a tie, sustains the chair on the principle that only a majority can reverse the decision of the chair.

It is a general rule that no one can vote on a question in which he or she has a direct personal or financial interest. However, a member can vote for himself or herself for any office or other position. A member can also vote when other members are included with him or her in a motion, even when the member has a personal or financial interest in the outcome, for instance a vote on charges made against more than one person, or on a resolution to increase the salaries of all the members. If a member were forbidden in all cases to vote on a question affecting himself or herself, it would be impossible for a society to vote to hold a banquet, for a legislature to vote salaries to members, or for the majority to prevent a small minority from preferring charges against them and suspending or expelling them. Simply by including the names of all members, except those of their own faction, in a resolution preferring charges against a majority, a minority could seize control were it not for the fact that in such a case all members are entitled to vote regardless of their personal interest. A sense of propriety usually prevents a member from exercising this right to vote in matters affecting himself except where his or her vote might affect the result. When charges are preferred against a member and the assembly has ordered the member to appear for trial, he or she is technically under arrest and is deprived of all rights of membership. The member therefore cannot vote until his or her case is disposed of.

Members have the right to change their votes at any time before the final vote is announced. Afterward, changes can only be made with the assembly's permission. This may be given by general consent (i.e., if, when the chair inquires, no member objects). If objection is made, a motion may be made to grant the permission. This motion is undebatable.

It is the duty of every member who has an opinion on a question to express it by his or her vote, but no member can be compelled to vote. Knowing beforehand which side will prevail, the member may prefer to abstain.

Voting by Ballot. Secrecy is the main object of this form of voting. It is resorted to when the question is one on which some members might hesitate to vote publicly their true feelings. Its special use is in the reception of members, elections and trials of members and officers, as well as in the preliminary steps in both cases. The by-laws should require the vote to be by ballot in such cases. Where the by-laws do not require the vote to be by ballot, this can be ordered by a majority vote or by general consent. Such motions are undebatable. Voting by ballot is almost never used in legislative bodies, but in ordinary societies, especially secret ones, it is often used for elections and trials, and sometimes for the selection of the next place for the meeting of a convention. As the usual object of the ballot is secrecy, when the by-laws require the vote to be taken by ballot any motion is out of order that members cannot oppose without exposing their views on the question to be decided by ballot. Thus, it is out of order to move that one person cast the ballot of the assembly for a certain person when the by-laws require the vote to be by ballot. When the ballot is not unanimous, it is out of order to move to make the vote unanimous, unless the motion is voted on by ballot to allow members to vote against it in secrecy.

When the question can be answered ***yes*** or ***no***, sometimes black balls, white balls, and a ballot box are provided for voting. The white ball answers ***yes***, and the black one ***no.*** In ordinary deliberative assemblies the ballots are strips of paper upon which are printed or written *yes* or *no* or the names of the candidates, as the case may be. After the ballots have been distributed, tellers collect them. The voting members remain in their seats, dropping their ballots into a hat or a box. Alternatively, the members come to the ballot box and hand their folded ballot to a teller, who deposits it. In the latter case the tellers must see that no member votes twice. In large societies this is best done by checking off the names from a list of members as the ballots are deposited. The ballots should usually be folded. If more than one is voted by the same person the tellers will detect it in unfolding the ballot. Furthermore, if ballots are not folded, when the tellers collect them, watchful that members vote only once, votes may be exposed.

When everyone appears to have voted, the chair asks, "Have all voted who wish to?" If there is no response the chair says, "The polls are closed." The tellers then count the ballots. In unfolding the ballots, if they find two folded together, they reject both as fraudulent. A blank piece of paper is not counted as a ballot and does not cause the rejection of the ballot with which it was folded. Blanks are ignored. Members who do not wish to vote can use this method to conceal the fact. Errors such as the misspelling of a word should be ignored if the meaning of the ballot is clear. In all cases where the name on the ballot sounds like the name of one of the candidates it should be so credited. If a ballot is written *Johnson* or *Johnston* or *Johnstone*, it should be credited to the candidate whose name is one of these. If there are two candidates with these names and no eligible member with the name on the ballot, it must be rejected as illegal or reported to the chair, who immediately submits the question to the assembly as to whom the ballot should be credited. If doubtful ballots do not affect the result, the tellers may make their full report without asking for instructions in regard to them, placing the doubtful votes opposite the name as written on the ballot. Votes for ineligible persons and fraudulent votes should be reported after the legal votes under the heading of

Illegal Votes. Two or more filled-out ballots that are folded together are counted as one fraudulent vote. The names of the candidates should be arranged in order. The candidate who receives the highest number of legal votes is listed first. In reporting the number of votes cast and the number necessary for election, all votes except blanks must be counted. Suppose the tellers find one hundred ballot papers, four of which are blank. One contains two filled-out ones folded together, and fifty are cast for a person who is ineligible because of having held the office as long as permitted by the constitution; the teller's report should be in this form:

Number of votes cast 96

Necessary for election 49

Ms. A received 37

Mr. B received 8

Illegal Votes.

Ms. C (ineligible) received 50

One ballot containing two for Mr. D, folded together, rejected as fraudulent 1

The head teller stands, addresses the chair, reads the report, hands it to the chair, and takes his or her seat, without saying who is elected. The chair rereads the teller's report and declares who is elected. In the case given above, the chair would declare no election, and state the reason. If no one is elected, another ballot must be taken. Balloting continues until there is an election. The chair should always vote in case of a ballot. When the chair fails to vote before the ballots are closed, he or she must have the permission of the assembly to do so. When the tellers report, they should hand the ballots to the secretary, who should hold them until it is certain that the assembly will not order a recount, which it may do by a majority vote.

Yeas and Nays, [1] or ***Roll Call.*** When a vote has been ordered to be taken by yeas and nays [See **25** for the motion] the chair puts the question in this form: "As many as are in favor of the adoption of these resolutions will, as their names are called, answer yes [or ***yea***]; those opposed will answer no [or ***nay***]." The chair then directs the clerk to call the roll. The negative is put at the same time as the affirmative. After one member has answered the roll call, it is too late to renew the debate. The clerk calls the roll and each member, as his or her name is called, rises and answers **"yes"** or **"no,"** or **"present"** if he or she does not wish to vote. The clerk notes the answers in separate columns. When the roll call is completed, the clerk reads the names of those who answered in the affirmative, then of those in the negative, and finally those who answered ***present.*** Mistakes may then be corrected. The clerk then gives the number voting on each side to the chair, who announces the result. An entry must be made in the minutes of the names of all voting in the affirmative, and also of those in the negative, and those who answered **"present."** A convenient method of noting the answers at the roll call is to write the figure 1 on the left of the name of the first member answering in the affirmative, the figure 2 to the left of the second name in the affirmative, and so on. The negative answers are treated similarly, being entered to the right of the names. Those answering ***present*** should be entered similarly in a third column. In this way the last number on each side shows where the vote stands at any time. The ***yeas and nays*** cannot be ordered in committee of the whole.

General Consent. When the formality of motions and voting can be avoided in routine business and on questions of little importance, business can be handled with greater efficiency, the chair assuming general (unanimous) consent until someone objects. General consent does not necessarily mean that every member is in favor of the motion, but, knowing it is useless to oppose it or even to discuss it, the opposition simply acquiesces in the formality. Thus, in the case of approving the minutes, the chair asks if there are any corrections. If one is suggested, it is made. When no correction is suggested, the chair says, **"There being no corrections** [or **no further corrections**] **the minutes stand approved."** While routine and minor matters can be rapidly disposed of in this way, any time an objection is made promptly, the chair ignores what has been done even if he has announced the result, and requires a regular vote. [See **48.**]

Absentee Voting. In a strictly deliberative assembly no member can vote who is not present when the question is completely put. However, in many societies the membership is scattered across a wider distance. It is then useful to provide a method of voting that enables all members to vote on certain matters, on amendments to constitutions and by-laws, and in elections of officers, for example. When it is deemed advisable to adopt it, this provision should be placed in the constitution or by-laws. Otherwise, unless the charter or state laws authorize absentee voting, members can vote only in person. There are two forms of absentee voting—by mail, and proxy voting.

Voting by Mail is used for election of officers, for amendments to the constitution or by-laws, and for other important matters that the society may order to be voted on in this way. If an amendment to the by-laws is to be voted on by mail, a printed copy of the proposed amendment is mailed to every member, with the words *yes* and *no* printed underneath or on a separate slip with directions to cross out one of them and return it in an enclosed envelope upon which should be printed the words ***Ballot for Amendment to the Constitution.*** This envelope should usually bear the signature of the voter and be sealed and enclosed in another one addressed to the secretary or to the chair of the tellers, so that the inner envelope will not be opened except by the tellers when the votes are counted. If it is desired to present the arguments pro and con, the society can allow the leaders on the two sides to prepare brief statements to be printed and mailed with the proposed amendment to every member. Instead of having the voter's signature on the inner envelope, it may be placed on the ballot, but a place for the signature should be indicated, so that there may be some means to guard against votes being cast by other than legal voters. Because it is necessary for the tellers to know by whom each vote is cast, voting by mail cannot be a secret ballot. By a method similar to this it is thus possible to give all members, however scattered they may be, an opportunity to vote on matters of great importance.

Proxy Voting. A proxy is a power of attorney given by one person to another to vote in his or her place. It is also used to designate the person who holds the power of attorney. It is unknown to a strictly deliberative assembly and is in conflict with the fundamental principle of the equality of members. There can be little use for debate when one member has more votes than another, and possibly more than all the others combined. With two limitations, proxy voting can be useful and do no harm. These limitations are: ***(1)*** *Proxy voting should be limited to the election of a board of directors,* as is essentially the case in stock corporations; ***(2)*** *Proxies must be given to members of the cor-*

poration in all cases where an election is required for membership.

In stock companies the members meet only annually to elect directors who elect the officers and transact the business of the corporation. Though the directors are elected largely by proxies, their own meetings, where all the busines is done, are as secret as they choose to make them. No proxies are allowed in them, and proxy voting therefore does not interfere with their business. As anyone can dispose of his stock to anyone else, there is no objection to his appointing anyone as his proxy.

The case is very different with many incorporated societies of a social, benevolent, or religious character, whose business meetings are sometimes secret, and whose members cannot transfer their membership like stock and should not be allowed to appoint any proxies who are not members of the organization. State law is above the by-laws of the society. If state law empowers members of all corporations to appoint proxies to vote at all business meetings, no by-laws of an incorporated secret society can prevent non-members holding proxies from attending and voting at all business meetings of the society.

This should not be the case. With stock corporations it does no harm, because all the business is done by directors, and no proxies are allowed in their meetings where no one can be present without their consent. But in many societies of the kind mentioned the business is transacted in meetings attended by none but members, and unlimited proxies would be a serious interference with their work. If the state law requires proxy voting in all corporations, it should be limited to the election of officers, including directors. Also, in all organizations whose primary object is not financial profit, it should be required that only members of the organization hold the proxies.

47. Votes that are Null and Void even if Unanimous. No motion is in order that conflicts with the laws of the nation or state, or with the assembly's constitution or by-laws. Such motions, even if adopted by a unanimous vote, are null and void. No rule that conflicts with a rule of a higher order is of any authority.

A by-law providing for the suspension by general consent of an article of the constitution is null and void.

The general parliamentary rule allowing a two-thirds vote to amend the by-laws after due notice is only in force when the by-laws are silent on the subject.

Rules that protect absentees cannot be suspended informally by general consent, or formally by a unanimous vote, because the absentees have not given their consent. For instance, a rule requiring the giving of a specified notice of certain motions, as an amendment of the by-laws, cannot be suspended by general consent or by a unanimous vote.

When a ballot vote is required, the object is to enable members to conceal their votes. Any motion that defeats this object is out of order. Thus, when the rules require the vote to be by ballot, as is usual in elections to office or membership, this rule cannot be suspended even by general consent, because no one can object without exposing his or her vote, which he or she cannot be compelled to do.

When the election must be by ballot, a motion to have the ballot cast by one person is out of order. When the rules require the vote to be by ballot, a motion to make unanimous a vote that was not unanimous must be voted on by ballot. Otherwise the vote would not be secret.

48. Motions requiring more than a Majority Vote.

Majority Vote. Any legitimate motion—other than those noted below that require more than a majority vote, requires for its adoption only a majority (i.e., more than half of the votes cast, ignoring blanks, at a legal meeting where a quorum is present), unless the rules of the assembly require a larger vote for its adoption.

General Consent or Unanimous Vote. By general, unanimous, or silent consent, the assembly can do business with little regard for the rules of procedure. These rules are made for the protection of the minority. When there is no minority to protect, there is little use for the restraint of the rules, except those that protect the rights of absent members or the right to a secret vote. In the former case the consent of the absentees cannot be given. In the latter case the consent cannot be withheld by the minority without exposing their votes, which they cannot be compelled to do. When the election is not by ballot and there are several candidates, one of whom receives a majority vote, a motion is sometimes made to make the vote unanimous. This should only be made by the runner-up candidate or by his representative. Even then the propriety of such a motion is dubious. One negative vote defeats a motion to make a vote unanimous, just as a single objection defeats a request for general consent.

Business can be greatly expedited by the legitimate use of the principle that rules designed for the protection of the minority do not need to be strictly enforced when there is no minority to protect. When there is evidently no opposition, the formality of voting can be avoided by the chair's asking if there is any objection to the proposed action, and if there is none, announcing the result. The action thus taken is said to be done by general consent, or unanimous or silent consent. Thus, after an order has been adopted limiting speeches to two minutes each, if a speaker is so interesting that there is a general demand that he or she continue beyond the time, the chair, instead of waiting for a motion and taking a vote, may accept it as the assembly's will that the time be extended. Or, the chair might say that if there is no objection the speaker's time will be extended for a specified time. [See also *General Consent*, **46**.]

Two-thirds Vote means ***two-thirds of the votes cast,*** ignoring blanks, which should never be counted. This must not be confused with a vote of two-thirds of the members present, or two-thirds of the members, terms sometimes used in by-laws. Suppose 14 members vote on a question in a meeting of a society where 20 are present out of a total membership of 70, a two-thirds vote would be 10; a two-thirds vote of the members present would be 14; and a vote of two-thirds of the members would be 47.

As a compromise between the rights of the individual and the rights of the assembly stands the principle that a two-thirds vote is required to adopt any motion that **(a)** *suspends or modifies a rule of order previously adopted;* **(b)** *prevents the introduction of a question for consideration;* **(c)** *closes, or limits, or extends the limits of debate;* **(d)** *limits the freedom of nomination or voting;* **(e)** *closes nominations or the polls;* or **(f)** *deprives one of membership or office.*

Every motion in the following list belongs to one of the above classes. ***Motions Requiring a Two-thirds Vote:***[2] **(a)** *Amend (Annul, Repeal, or Rescind) any part of the Constitution, By-laws, or Rules of Order, previ-*

ously adopted (this also requires previous notice) **[68]**; ***(b)*** *Amend or Rescind a Standing Rule, a Program or Order of Business, or a Resolution, previously adopted, without notice being given at a previous meeting or in the call for the meeting* **[37]**; ***(c)*** *Take up a Question out of its Proper Order* **[22]**; ***(d)*** *Suspend the Rules* **[22]**; ***(e)*** *Make a Special Order* **[20]**; ***(f)*** *Discharge an Order of the Day before it is Pending* **[20]**; ***(g)*** *Refuse to Proceed to the Orders of the Day* **[20]**; ***(h)*** *Sustain an Objection to the Consideration of a Question* **[23]**; ***(i)*** *Previous Question* **[29]**; ***(j)*** *Limit, or Extend the Limits, of Debate* **[30]**; ***(k)*** *Extend the Time Appointed for Adjournment or for Taking a Recess* **[20]**; ***(l)*** *Close Nominations* **[26]** *or the Polls* **[25]**; ***(m)*** *Limit the Names to be Voted for*; ***(n)*** *Expel from Membership* (this also requires previous notice) *and trial* **[75]**; ***(o)*** *Depose from Office* (this also requires previous notice); ***(p)*** *Discharge a Committee when previous notice has not been given* **[32]**; ***(q)*** *Reconsider in Committee when a member of the majority is absent and has not been notified of the proposed reconsideration* **[36.]**

Article IX: Committees and Boards

49. **COMMITTEES CLASSIFIED**
50. **BOARDS OF MANAGERS OR DIRECTORS, BOARDS OF TRUSTEES, EXECUTIVE COMMITTEES, ETC.**
51. **EX-OFFICIO MEMBERS OF BOARDS AND COMMITTEES**
52. **COMMITTEES, SPECIAL AND STANDING**
53. **RECEPTION OF REPORTS**
54. **ADOPTION OR ACCEPTANCE OF REPORTS**
55. **COMMITTEE OF THE WHOLE**
56. **AS IF IN (OR QUASI) COMMITTEE OF THE WHOLE**
57. **INFORMAL CONSIDERATION**

49. Committees Classified. A committee is a body of one or more persons appointed or elected by an assembly or society to do any or all of the following things: to consider, investigate, or take action in regard to certain matters or subjects. Committees may be divided into two distinct classes: *(1) Boards of Managers or Directors, Boards of Trustees, Executive Committees, etc; (2) Ordinary Committees, Special or Standing*

Committees, and Committee of the Whole and Its Substitutes. These different kinds of committees are considered separately in the following three sections.

50. Boards of Managers or Directors, Boards of Trustees, Executive Committees, etc. Committees of this class are essentially small deliberative assemblies subordinate to the body that appoints them. Their duties, authority, the number of their regular meetings, and their quorums are defined by the parent body or by its authority. Boards or Committees of this class are usually appointed by organizations that meet only annually or quarterly. Such organizations customarily and necessarily delegate to a committee, usually known as the Board of Managers or Directors, all their authority, with slight limitations, to be exercised between its meetings. The by-laws of the board are adopted by the parent body. The board may sometimes be authorized to adopt its own by-laws. It is usual to authorize the board to appoint from its membership an Executive Committee of a specified number who shall have all the power of the board between the meetings of the board, just as the board has all the power of the society between the meetings of the society. The subordinate body, however, cannot modify any action taken by its superior. The Executive Committee should be small. Its members should live near enough to each other to be able to have frequent regular meetings and special emergency meetings. Where the organization is local, such as a local charitable society, the Board of Managers usually divides itself into committees that are assigned different branches of the work during the intervals between the monthly or quarterly meetings of the board when these committees report on the work done. Resolutions or other matters are rarely referred to boards or committees of this class for them to report back to the society with recommendations. Papers are usually referred to them only for their information and for action. They are organized as any other deliberative assembly with a chairman and a secretary, whom they elect if they are not appointed by the society. The by-laws of the society often make its president and its corresponding or executive secretary, ex-officio **[51]** president and secretary of the Board of Managers.

In large boards business is transacted just as in the society meetings. In small boards the same formality is neither necessary nor usual, and the informality observed by committees is generally allowed. In a board meeting where fewer than a dozen are present, for instance, it is unnecessary to rise to make a motion, to wait for recognition by the chair before speaking or making a motion, or to second a motion. There is no need to limit the number of speeches, nor does the chair rise to make a motion or to discuss a question. The formalities required to transact business in a large assembly would hinder business in so small a body.

Boards are often constituted so that the term of office of, say, one-third of its members expires each year. After each annual meeting in such cases, the board elects new officers and committees, just as if the entire board had been re-elected. All unfinished business falls to the ground when the new board is elected.

The by-laws customarily require an annual report from the Board of Managers, which usually gives a brief account of its activities for the year with recommendations for the future. After discussion, and amendment if necessary, the report is usually adopted by the society and published in its annual proceedings as the report of the board. In publishing the report care should be taken to enclose in brackets all that has been struck out, to put in *italics* whatever has been inserted, and to insert a note explaining this at the beginning of the report. The board's exact recommendations can readily be seen when this is done. The minutes should read thus: "The Board of Managers submitted its report which after discussion and amendment was adopted as follows, the words in brackets having been struck out and those underscored (in *italics*) having been inserted before the report was adopted." The society can alter the report of the board. It may refuse to endorse it, or even to allow it to be printed, but it cannot make it appear that the board stated anything other than what it reported.

51. Ex-Officio Members of Boards and Committees. Members of boards and committees are often so by virtue of their office. The board membership of such persons, called ex-officio members, ends when they cease to hold office. If the ex-officio member is under the society's control, the only distinction between him or her and the other members is that the president is ex-officio member of all committees. Here the intention is to permit, but not to require, the president to act as a member of the various committees. In counting a quorum he or she therefore should not be counted as a member. Unless the president is so appointed by the assembly, he or she is not a member of any committee except by virtue of a special rule. An ex-officio member who is not under the authority of the society has all the privileges, including the right to vote, but none of the obligations of membership (as when the governor of a state is, ex-officio, a trustee of a private school).

52. Committees, Special and Standing. Committees usually do all preliminary work in the preparation of matter for the action of deliberative assemblies. The committee may be a ***standing committee*** appointed for a definite time, a session or a year; a ***special*** (or ***select***) ***committee*** appointed for a special purpose; or a ***committee of the whole*** consisting of the entire assembly. [For the method of appointing

Committees of the Whole, see **55**; other committees, see *Commit*, **32**.] *Committees of the Whole* are rarely used except in legislative bodies. [The word *committee* in this manual refers to ***standing*** or ***special*** committees unless noted otherwise.] Unless the assembly has appointed a chair, either directly or through its presiding officer, the first named on a committee, and in his or her absence the next named member and so on, becomes chair and should act as such unless the committee elects a chair by majority vote. It has the right to do this (standing committees usually do) if the assembly has not appointed one. The clerk should furnish the committee chair, or in his or her absence another committee member, with notice of the appointment of the committee, the names of the members, the papers or matter referred to it, and the assembly's instructions. On the committee's request, all papers and books necessary for the proper performance of its duties should be turned over to it by the proper officers.

It is the chair's duty to call the committee together. If he or she is absent or neglects or declines to call a meeting of the committee, the committee must meet on the call of any two of its members. The chair usually acts as secretary in small special committees. In large ones and all standing committees, it is customary to elect a secretary who keeps for the committee's use a brief memorandum of what is done. Members of the society are entitled to appear at committee meetings to present their views on the subject before it at reasonable times the committee appoints on request. During committee deliberations, however, only the members of the committee have the right to be present.

Where possible, the rules of the assembly apply to the committee. Motions to close or limit debate are not allowed, however, and there is no limit to the number of times a member may speak. It is unnecessary for anyone to rise and address the chair before making a motion or speaking. The chair neither rises to put the question nor leaves the chair to speak or make motions. Motions are not seconded. These formalities are rarely necessary unless the committee is very large. Unless agreed to by general consent, all questions must be put to vote. Rather than abstaining from speaking on questions, the chair is usually the most active participant in the discussions and work of the committee. In order that the assembly may have the benefit of the matured judgment of the committee, a reconsideration of a vote must be allowed regardless of time and previous reconsideration. This may be moved by anyone who does not vote with the minority, even if he or she was absent when the previous vote was taken. Its adoption requires a two-thirds vote unless every member who voted with the majority is either present or received ample notice of the meeting and that the reconsideration was to be moved. This prevents taking advantage of the absence of members to reverse action, and enables members who were absent to bring up the question of reconsideration.

The committee constitutes a miniature assembly. It can act only when a quorum (a majority of the members) is present. If a paper is referred to them, they must not write on it, but should write their amendments on a separate sheet. When amendments are numerous it is better to write out and submit a substitute. If a resolution is referred to a committee when a motion to postpone indefinitely is pending, only the resolution is referred to them. The motion to postpone indefinitely is ignored. Pending amendments go to the committee, which recommend their adoption or rejection, or make no recommendation in regard to them. If the committee originates the paper, all amendments must be incorporated in it. When they originate it, usually one member has prepared a draft beforehand. This is read in its entirety, and then read by paragraphs, the chair pausing after each paragraph and asking, **"Are there any amendments proposed to this paragraph?"** No vote is taken on the adoption of the separate paragraphs. After the entire paper has been read in this way, it is open to amendment generally, by striking out any paragraph, or by substituting or inserting new ones, or by substituting an entirely new paper for it. If there is a preamble, it is considered last. When the entire paper has been amended to the committee's satisfaction, they should adopt it as their report and direct the chair or another member to report it to the assembly. When committees are appointed to investigate or to report on certain matters, the report should close with, or be accompanied by, formal resolutions covering all recommendations, so that when their report is made the only motion necessary is to adopt the resolutions.

If the report is written in this form: **"Your committee is of the opinion that Mr. K's bill should be paid,"** there might be some doubt as to the effect of the adoption of the recommendation or the report. The report should close with a recommendation that the following order be adopted: **"Ordered, That the Treasurer pay Mr. K's bill for $5,000.00."** If a report recommends that charges be preferred against Mr. L, it should close with recommending the adoption of resolutions. These should be written out, should provide for holding an adjourned meeting, and should cite the member to appear at the adjourned meeting for trial on charges that must be specified. These should be prepared by the committee and submitted as part of their report. The committee should never leave to others the responsibility of preparing resolutions to carry out their recommendations. They should consider this as one of their most important duties.

When the report has been adopted by the committee, a clear copy is made, usually beginning in a style similar to this: **"The committee to whom was referred** [state the matter referred] **beg leave to submit the following report,"** or **"Your committee appointed**

to [specify the object] **respectfully report,"** etc. If the report is important it should be signed by all the members who agree to it. When it is of little importance or when it merely recommends amendments, etc., it may be signed by the chair alone, his or her signature being followed by the word ***Chair***. He or she should place ***Chair*** after his or her signature only when signing the report alone and by the committee's authority. Though written and signed by only one, the report must always be in the third person. The signature may be preceded by the words ***Respectfully submitted,*** but this is not required. Usually the report is not dated or addressed. It sometimes consists merely of a resolution, or a set of resolutions. In the latter case the chair states that he or she is instructed by the committee to submit and to move the adoption of the resolutions. The report of the majority is the report of the committee and should never be referred to as the majority report.

If the minority submit a report (more properly, their "views"), it may begin thus: "The undersigned, a minority of the committee appointed, etc., not agreeing with the majority, desire to express their views in the case." After the committee's report has been read, the motion to adopt has been made, and the question stated, it is usual to allow the minority to present their views. If anyone objects to its reception the chair should put the question to vote on its being received. A majority vote is required to receive it, and the question is undebatable. The minority report is read only for information. It can only be acted upon by a motion to substitute it for the report of the committee. Whether the views of the minority are read or not, anyone can move to substitute the resolutions they recommend for those recommended by the committee. Where the minority cannot agree, each member may submit his or her views separately. A member sometimes agrees to the report with a single exception. In this case, the member does not submit his or her views separately. After everyone in agreement with the report signs it, the member may write that he or she agrees to it except the part specified and then sign it.

The committee's report[1] can contain only what has been agreed to by a majority vote at a meeting of which every member has been notified, or at an adjourned meeting where a quorum (a majority of the members) is present. When it is impracticable for the committee to meet, its entire membership must agree to the report. When a committee is appointed from different sections of the country with the expectation that its work will be done by correspondence, its report can contain only what is agreed to by a majority of the members.

A committee (but not a committee of the whole) can appoint a subcommittee. It reports only to the committee, never to the assembly. This subcommittee must consist of members of the committee, except when it is appointed to take action that requires the assistance of others, as to make arrangements for holding a banquet. In such cases it is best to appoint the subcommittee with power to appoint any required subcommittees; or, as is often done, to appoint the committee ***with power***. This means with power to take all steps necessary to carry out its instructions.

A committee has no power to punish its members for disorderly conduct. It may report the facts to the assembly. Only by a report of the committee or by general consent can any allusion can be made in the assembly to what has occurred during the deliberations of the committee.

When a special committee has completed its work, a motion is made for the committee to ***rise***. This is equivalent to the motion to adjourn without day. The chair or some member who is more familiar with the subject then presents the committee's report to the assembly. As soon as the assembly receives its report, a special committee ceases to exist.

When a committee adjourns without appointing a time for the next meeting, it is considered as having adjourned at the call of the chair, so that all the meetings of a special committee constitute one session. A meeting of a special committee may be called at any time by the chair or by any two of its members, every member being notified. When a committee adjourns to meet at another time, it is unnecessary, though usually advisable, to notify absent members of the adjourned meeting.

A *standing committee* is either wholly or partially elected at each annual meeting in ordinary societies. It reorganizes immediately afterward, electing a chair (unless he or she has been appointed by the assembly) and a secretary. A standing committee must therefore report at the annual meeting, or before, on everything referred to it during the year. The motion to rise is never used in standing committees or boards. It is used in other committees only when they are ready to report and will never meet again. A special committee is appointed for a specific purpose. Unless discharged beforehand, which requires a two-thirds vote when done without notice, it continues to exist until the duty assigned to it by the society is accomplished. An intervening annual meeting does not discharge a special committee appointed by a society. In an elected or appointed body such as a convention, special committees that have not reported cease to exist when the new officers assume their duties at the next annual meeting. When discharged, the chair of the committee returns to the secretary all documents received from him or her.

Committees are rarely necessary in small assemblies, especially in those where little business is done. In large assemblies or in those doing a great deal of business, committees are extremely important. When a committee is properly selected, in nine cases out of ten its action decides that of the assembly. A committee for ***action*** should be small and should consist only of those who heartily favor the proposed action. An appointee who disapproves the proposed action should ask to be excused. On the contrary, a committee for deliberation or investigation should be large and representative of all parties in the assembly. The committee's opinion then has more authority. The committee's usefulness is greatly impaired when any important faction of the assembly is unrepresented on the committee. The appointment of a committee is fully explained in **32**.

53. Reception of Reports. When a place is provided in the order of business for committee reports, they are not made until they are called for by the chair. When the time arrives, the chair calls for the reports of such officers and standing committees as are required to make them, in the order in which they are arranged in the rules. The chair then calls for the reports of the special committees in the order of their appointment. When called upon, the reporting member (the committee chair unless another member is appointed to make the report) rises and addresses the chair. When recognized, he or she reads the report and hands it to the chair or the secretary. When necessary, the reporting member moves the adoption or acceptance of the report [**54**]. If the committee reports back a paper with amendments, the amendments are read with sufficient of the related parts to make them understood. To make a report earlier than the rules allow, the rules can be suspended by a two-thirds vote [22] to receive the report immediately.

When the order of business does not provide for the committee report, the reporting member, when ready, obtains the floor when no business is pending, and informs the assembly that the committee to which was referred the subject or paper has agreed upon a report that he or she is now prepared to submit. If of the opinion that the assembly wishes to hear the report, the chair directs the reporting member to proceed. He or she then reads the report, hands it to the chair, and makes the proper motion for its disposal. If before it is read anyone objects to its reception, or if the chair questions whether it should be received at once, the chair puts to the assembly the question **"Shall the report be received now?"** This question is undebatable. A majority vote is required to receive the report. If the vote is negative, a time for the reception of the report should be appointed either by a vote or by general consent. Usually, these matters are settled informally by general consent, and no motions are made or votes taken in regard to receiving reports.

The work of the committee is completed when the assembly receives its final report. The committee is then automatically discharged from further consideration of the subject. If it is a special committee, it ceases to exist. If the report is incomplete, the committee is not discharged unless the assembly so votes. If the subject is recommitted, the committee is revived (unless the reference is to another committee) and all parts of the report that have not been adopted by the assembly are ignored by the committee as if the report had never been made. If any member or members wish to submit the views of the minority, such views are customarily heard immediately after receiving the report of the committee. In such cases the reporting member should notify the assembly that the views of the minority will be submitted in a separate paper. As soon as the chair has stated the question on the report, he or she should call for the views of the minority. These are then read for information. They are only acted upon when it is moved to substitute the recommendations of the minority for those of the committee.

Moving that a report be ***received*** after it has been read is a common error. That it has been read shows that the assembly has already received it. Another mistake, less common but dangerous, is to vote that the report be ***accepted***. This is equivalent to ***adopting*** it when often the intention is only to have the report up for consideration and *afterward* to vote on its adoption.

54. Adoption or Acceptance of Reports. When the report of a committee has been received (i.e., presented to the assembly and either read or handed to the chair or the secretary), the next business in order is the disposal of the report, the proper disposition depending upon its nature: ***(1) If the report contains only a statement of fact or opinion for the information of the assembly,*** the reporting member makes no motion for its disposal, as no action on the report is needed. If any action is taken, the proper motion (which should be made by someone else) is to ***accept the report.*** This endorses the statement and makes the assembly assume responsibility for it.

If it is a financial report, as in the case of a board of trustees or a treasurer, it should be referred to an auditing committee. The vote to accept the report does not endorse the accuracy of the figures. The assembly can only be sure of that by having the report audited. Whenever such a financial report is made, the chair without any motion should say it is referred to the auditing committee or auditors, if there are any. If there are none, then the proper motion is to refer it to an auditing committee to be appointed by the chair. When the auditing committee reports, this report should be accepted or adopted. This carries with it endorsement of the financial report.

(2) If the report contains recommendations that are not in the form of motions, they should all be placed at the end of the report, even if they have been given separately before. The proper motion is to adopt the recommendations.

(3) If the report concludes with a resolution or a series of resolutions, the reporting member should move that the resolution or resolutions be adopted or agreed to. This procedure should be followed whenever possible.

(4) If a committee reports back a resolution that was referred to it, the motion to postpone indefinitely, if it was pending, is ignored. If an amendment was pending it should be reported on. The form of the question to be stated by the chair depends upon the recommendation of the committee as follows. ***(4a) If the committee recommends its adoption, or makes no recommendation (where it can come to no agreement),*** the question should be stated on the amendment if there was one pending, and then on the resolution. These motions were pending when the question was referred to the committee, and therefore should not be made again. ***(4b) If the committee recommends the rejection of the resolution,*** the question on the resolution, when it is put, should be stated thus: "The question is on the adoption of the resolution, the recommendation of the committee to the contrary notwithstanding." A similar course is pursued if the committee recommends the rejection of an amendment. ***(4c) If the committee recommends that the resolution be postponed indefinitely, or postponed to a certain time,*** the question should be on the postponement. If that is lost, the question is then on the resolution. ***(4d) If the committee reports back a resolution or paper with amendments,*** the reporting member reads only the amendments with sufficient of the context to make them understood and then moves their adoption. After stating the question on the adoption of the amendments, the chair calls for the reading of the first one, which then is open for debate and amendment. After a vote is taken on adopting this amendment, the next is read, and so on until all are adopted or rejected, admitting amendments to the committee's amendments but no others. When through with the committee's amendments, the chair pauses for any other amendments to be proposed by the assembly. After these are voted on, he or she puts the question on adopting the paper as amended, unless, in a case like revising the by-laws, they have already been adopted. A report can be immediately adopted without following this routine by suspending the rules [22] or by general consent. If the amendments do not call for debate or amendment, as when reported from the committee of the whole where they have been already discussed, the chair puts a single question on all the committee's amendments except those for which a member asks a separate vote, thus: "As many as are in favor of adopting the amendments recommended by the committee, except those for which a separate vote has been asked, say aye; those opposed say no." The chair then takes up the remaining amendments separately in their order. ***(4e) If the committee reports back a resolution with a substitute that it recommends for adoption,*** the chair states the question on the substitute if there were no amendments pending when the resolution was committed. If, however, amendments were pending when the resolution was committed, the chair first states the questions on those pending amendments. When they are disposed of, the chair states the question on the substitute. In either case the substitute is treated like any other substitute motion. The resolution is first perfected by amendments and then the substitute resolution. When both are perfected the question is put on the substitution, and finally on the resolution. If the substitute is lost the resolution is open to amendments. ***(4f) If the report is of a nomination committee,*** no vote should be taken, any more than if a member had made the nominations. ***(4g) If the report is from the membership committee,*** the chair immediately states the question on accepting into membership the candidates recommended by the committee.

A committee's partial report is treated like the final report. If it reports progress only, with no recommendations or conclusions, it is treated as any other report for information. No action is necessary. If the partial report recommends action, the question is put on adopting the report, its recommendations or the resolutions, just as if it were the final report.

The usual practice in ordinary societies is to make and second a motion to accept or adopt a committee's report. However, if a motion is not made and the chair thinks it best to have a vote taken on the question, he or she may state the appropriate question without waiting for a motion. The chair accepts the submission of the committee report as equivalent to moving the adoption of the appropriate motion for disposing of it, just as when one offers a resolution. It is pointless to wait to see if two members are in favor of a proposition that at least two have signed, or authorized the chair or the reportng member to sign. In ordinary societies the chair of the assembly usually knows better than the reporting member how business should be managed, especially if a resolution is reported with many amendments. However, unless the assembly is accustomed to having its chair put the proper questions on the report without any formal motion, it is generally assumed that the reporting member should move the ***adoption*** of the resolutions or recommendations.

When the chair has stated the question on the adoption of the recommendations or resolutions, or of the report, the matter under consideration is open to debate and amendment. Like other main questions, it may have any of the subsidiary motions applied to it. If the matter was referred to the committee, no one can object to its consideration.

While the assembly can amend the report of the committee or its resolutions, these amendments only affect what the assembly adopts. The assembly cannot in any way change the committee's report. For example, a committee expresses the opinion that Mr. A has no right to commit a certain act, and the assembly strikes this statement from the report before adopting it. This does not alter the report, but the statement is not adopted when the assembly adopts the report. It is thus with a recommendation or a resolution. The assembly may strike out or add one or more recommendations or resolutions before adoption, but this does not alter the committee's report. If the proceedings are published, the committee's report should be printed exactly as it was submitted, with the amendments printed below. Better still, all words struck out should be enclosed in brackets and all words inserted should be printed in *italics,* with a note explaining this inserted at the beginning.

55. Committee of the Whole. When an assembly must consider a subject that it does not wish to refer to a committee, although the subject matter is not well digested and put into proper form for definite action, or when for any other reason it is desirable for the assembly to consider a subject with all the freedom of an ordinary committee, the practice is often to refer the matter to the ***Committee of the Whole.*** If it is desired to consider the question immediately, the motion is made **"That the assembly do now resolve itself into a committee of the whole, to take under consideration,"** etc., or **"That we go into committee of the whole to consider,"** etc., specifying the subject. This is really a motion to ***commit.*** [See **32** for its order of precedence, etc.] If adopted, the chair immediately calls another member to the chair, and takes his place as a member of the committee. The committee is under the rules of the assembly, with the following exceptions: the only motions in order are to ***amend*** and to ***adopt,*** and that the committee ***rise and report.*** It cannot ***adjourn,*** nor can it order the ***yeas and nays.*** An appeal from the decision of the chair can be made and must be voted on directly. It cannot be laid on the table or postponed, because these motions are not allowed in committee of the whole. Each member can speak only once on the appeal. The only way to close or limit debate in committee of the whole is for the assembly, before going into committee of the whole, to vote that the debate in committee shall cease at a certain time, or that after a certain time debate shall be allowed only on new amendments with only one speech in favor and one against, each not to exceed, say, five minutes. The time for debate may be regulated in some other way, but this must be decided *before* going into committee of the whole.

If no time limit is prescribed, any member may speak as often as he or she can get the floor, and each time for as long as is allowed in debate in the assembly, but the member cannot speak a second time when another member wants the floor who has not spoken on the particular question. When debate has been closed at a particular time by order of the assembly, the committee has no power, even by unanimous consent, to extend the time. The committee cannot refer the subject to another committee. Like other committees, it cannot alter the text of any resolution referred to it. However, when the resolution originates in the committee, all the amendments are incorporated in it.

When the committee has completed consideration of the subject referred to it, or if it wishes to adjourn or to have the assembly limit debate, a motion is made that ***the committee rise and report,*** etc., specifying the result of its proceedings. The motion to ***rise*** is equivalent to the motion to ***adjourn*** in the assembly. It is in order unless a vote is being taken or another member has the floor. It cannot be debated or amended. As soon as this motion is adopted the presiding officer takes the chair, and the chair of the committee, having resumed his or her place in the assembly, rises, addresses the chair, and, if the committee has concluded its business, says: "The Committee of the Whole has had under consideration [here he or she describes the resolution or other matter] and has directed me to report the same with [or without] amendments." If the committee has failed to come to a conclusion, strike out of the report all after "and has" and insert "come to no conclusion thereon." If no amendments are reported, the chair at once states the question on the resolution or other matter referred to the committee. If amendments are reported the reporting member reads them, and hands the paper to the chair, who reads it, and states and puts the question on the amendments as a whole. A member can demand a separate vote on one or more amendments. In this case a single vote is first taken on all the other amendments. The question is then stated separately on each of the amendments for which a separate vote was demanded. The amendments may be debated and amended.

The secretary does not record in the minutes the proceedings of the committee, but should keep a memorandum of the proceedings for its use. In large assemblies the secretary leaves his or her seat, which is occupied by the chair of the committee, and the assistant secretary acts as secretary of the committee. If the committee becomes disorderly and the chair is unable to control it, the presiding officer should take the chair and declare the committee dissolved. The quorum of the committee of the whole is the same as that of the assembly [**64**]. If the committee finds itself without a quorum, it can only rise and report the fact to the assembly, which must then adjourn.

In large assemblies, such as the U.S. House of Representatives, where a member can speak to any question only once, the committee of the whole is almost a necessity. It allows the freest discussion of a subject, while at any time it can rise and thus bring into force the strict rules of the assembly. In small assemblies it is usually more convenient to substitute for it either ***As if in (or Quasi) Committee of the Whole,*** as used in the U.S. Senate, or ***Informal Consideration,*** as frequently used in ordinary societies. These are explained in the next two sections.

56. As if in (or Quasi) Committee of the Whole is used in the U.S. Senate instead of the committee of the whole. It is more convenient for small assemblies. The motion should be made in this form: "I move that the resolution be considered as if in committee of the whole." When this is adopted, the question is open to debate and amendment with all the freedom of the committee of the whole. The presiding officer, however, retains the chair, instead of appointing a chairman as is done when the assembly goes into committee of the whole. The quasi-committee of the whole is terminated if any motion other than an amendment is adopted. The motion to commit is thus equivalent to the following motions when in committee of the whole: *(1) that the committee **rise**; (2) that the committee of the whole be **discharged** from the further consideration of the subject;* and *(3) that it be **referred** to a committee.*

When the assembly has finished amending the proposition under consideration, without further motion the chair announces: "The assembly, acting as if in committee of the whole, has had such subject under consideration, and has made certain amendments," which he or she then reports. The subject then comes before the assembly as if reported by a committee. The chair states the question on the amendments. The secretary should keep a memorandum of the proceedings while acting ***as if in committee of the whole.*** This is for temporary use only and should not be entered in the minutes. The chair's report to the assembly should be entered in the minutes, as it belongs to the assembly's proceedings.

57. Informal Consideration. In ordinary societies whose meetings are not large, the practice of considering the question informally is more often used than going into committee of the whole, or considering questions as if in committee of the whole. The motion is made thus: **"I move that the question be considered informally."** The adoption of this motion opens the main question and any amendments that may be proposed to free debate as if in committee of the whole. No member can speak a second time to the same question when a member who has not spoken desires the floor. This informal consideration applies only to the main question and its amendments. The regular rules of debate govern any other motion that is made. When considering a question informally, the assembly by a two-thirds vote may limit the number or length of speeches, or in any other way limit or close the debate. Although the consideration of the main question and its amendments is informal, all votes are formal. The informality applies only to the number of speeches allowed in debate. The instant the main question is disposed of temporarily or permanently, the informal consideration automatically ceases without any motion or vote.

If a question is considered in either the regular committee of the whole or the quasi-committee of the whole, the action must be formally reported to the assembly which then must take action on the report. Informal consideration, thus, is much simpler than either of the methods described in **55** and **56**. It can be used to advantage in assemblies that are not very large, instead of the committee of the whole. While not a motion to commit, informal consideration is used for practically the same purpose as the committee of the whole. It ranks just below the motion to ***consider as if in committee of the whole,*** which is just below to ***go into committee of the whole.***

Article X: The Officers and the Minutes

58. Chair or President. The constitutions of organized societies always prescribe the title of the presiding officer, usually called the ***Chair,*** the ***President,*** or (especially in religious assemblies) the ***Moderator.*** The title of President is most often used. In debate he or she is referred to by official title and is addressed by prefixing ***Mr.*** or ***Madame*** to that title. He or she never uses the personal pronoun in referring to himself or herself, generally saying ***"the chair,"*** which means the presiding officer of the assembly regardless of whether his or her position is permanent or temporary. If the position is only temporary, the presiding officer is called the chair.

The duties of the chair are generally the following: ***(a)*** *to open the session when the assembly meets, by taking the chair and calling the members to order;* ***(b)*** *to announce the business before the assembly in the order* *in which it is to be acted upon* **[65]**; ***(c)*** *to recognize members entitled to the floor* **[3]**; ***(d)*** *to state* **[6]** *and to put to vote* **[9]** *all questions that are regularly moved, or necessarily arise in the course of the proceedings, and to announce the result of the vote;* ***(e)*** *to protect the assembly from annoyance from evidently frivolous or dilatory motions by refusing to recognize them* **[40]**; ***(f)*** *to assist in the expediting of business in every way compatible with the rights of the members, as by allowing brief remarks when undebatable motions are pending, if he or she thinks it advisable;* ***(g)*** *to restrain the members when engaged in debate, within the rules of order;* ***(h)*** *to enforce on all occasions the observance of order and decorum among the members, deciding all questions of order* (subject to an appeal to the assembly by any two members) *unless when in doubt he or she prefers to submit the question to the decision of the assembly* **[21]**; ***(i)*** *to inform the assembly, when necessary, or when referred to for the purpose, on a point of order or practice pertinent to pending business;* and ***(j)*** *to authenticate, by his or her signature, when necessary, all acts, orders, and proceedings of the assembly declaring its will and in all things obeying its commands.*

In case of very serious disorder, fire, riot, or any other great emergency, the chair has the right and the duty to declare the assembly adjourned to some other time (and place if necessary), if the taking of a vote is not practical, or the delay of taking one is in his or her opinion too dangerous.

Except in very small assemblies, such as boards or committees, the chair rises to put a question to vote, but he or she may state it sitting. The chair also rises (without calling anyone to the chair) when giving the reason for his or her decision upon a point of order, or when speaking upon an appeal, which the chair can do in preference to other members. During debate the chair should be seated and pay attention to the speaker, who is required to address his or her remarks to the presiding officer. The presiding officer should always refer to himself or herself as ***the chair:*** "the chair decides," not "I decide." When a member has the floor, the chair can interrupt the member only as provided in **3**, as long as the member does not transgress any of the rules of the assembly.

If the chair is a member of the assembly, he or she is entitled to vote when the vote is by ballot (but not after the tellers have begun to count the ballots), and in all other cases where the vote would change the result. Thus, when a two-thirds vote is necessary, and his or her vote thrown with the minority would prevent the adoption of the question, he or she can cast a vote. The chair can also vote with the minority when it will produce a tie vote and thus cause the motion to fail; but he or she cannot vote twice, first to make a tie, and then to give the casting vote. Whenever a motion is made referring to the chair only, or which compliments or condemns the chair with others, it should be put to vote by the vice president, the secretary, or by the maker of the motion. The chair should not hesitate to put the question on a motion to appoint delegates or a committee on account of his or her being included.

The chair can close debate only by order of the assembly. This requires a two-thirds vote. He or she cannot prevent the making of legitimate motions by hurrying through the proceedings. The chair cannot prevent reasonably prompt members from exercising their right to speak or make motions. If he or she quickly takes and announces a vote while a member is rising to address the chair, the vote is null and void, and the member must be recognized. The chair, however, should not permit the object of a meeting to be defeated by a few factious members using parliamentary forms with the evident object of obstructing business. In such a case the chair should refuse to recognize the dilatory or frivolous motion. The chair should entertain an appeal made to this, but, if he or she is sustained by a large majority, the chair may afterward refuse to entertain even an appeal made by the faction when evidently made to obstruct business. When the opposition is not factious, the chair should never adopt such a course merely to expedite business. It is only justifiable when it is perfectly clear that the opposition is trying to obstruct business. [See *Dilatory Motions,* **40.**]

If the presiding officer must leave the chair, the first vice president, if there is one, takes it. In his or her absence the next one in order does so. When there is no vice president in the hall and the presiding officer must leave the chair, he or she may appoint a chair *pro tem*. The first adjournment ends this appointment. The assembly can terminate it beforehand by electing another chair if it so wishes. The regular chair cannot authorize another member to act in his or her place at a future meeting that the chair knows he or she cannot attend. In this case, the secretary, if present, or some other member calls the meeting to order, and a chair *pro tem*. is elected to hold office during that session. The entrance of the president or a vice president terminates this office, or another chair *pro tem*. may be elected by majority vote.

In order to take part in debate, the chair sometimes calls a member to the chair. This is rarely wise. Nothing justifies this when a display of emotion creates any difficulty in preserving order. If the chair even appears to be partisan, he or she loses much of his or her ability to control those who are on the opposite side of the question. Nothing justifies the unfortunate habit some chairs have of constantly speaking on questions before the assembly, even interrupting the member who has the floor. One who expects to take an active part in debate should never accept the chair. At the very least, he or she should not resume the chair, after having made his or her speech, until after the pending question is disposed of.[1] The presiding officer of a large assembly should never be chosen for any reason except his or her ability to preside.

The chair should know parliamentary usage and set an example of strict conformity to it. He or she should also be a person of executive ability, capable of controlling men and women. The chair should set an example of courtesy, and should never forget that self-control is required of one who has the duty of controlling others. A nervous, excited chair can scarcely fail to cause trouble in a meeting. No rules take the place of tact and common sense on his or her part. While the chair usually need not wait for motions of routine, or for a motion to be seconded when he or she knows it is favored by others, when there is any objection to this, it is safer instantly to require the observance of the forms of parliamentary law. Many things can be done by general consent and this can save a lot of time [see **48**], but where the assembly is very large or is divided and contains members who are habitually raising points of order, the most certain and effective course is strictly to enforce all the rules and forms of parliamentary law. The chair should be particularly careful after every motion is made and every vote is taken to announce the next business in order. Whenever an improper motion is made, instead of simply ruling it out of order, the chair does well to suggest how the desired object can be accomplished. [See ***Hints to Inexperienced Presiding Officers,*** below.]

The by-laws sometimes state that the president shall

appoint all committees. In this case the assembly authorizes committees, but does not appoint or nominate them. The president cannot appoint any committees except those authorized by the by-laws or by a vote of the assembly. Sometimes the by-laws make the president an ***ex-officio*** member of every committee. Where this is done he or she has the rights of other members of the committees but not the obligation to attend every committee meeting. [See **51.**]

A presiding officer is often perplexed with the difficulties of his or her position. He or she will always do well to remember that parliamentary law was made for deliberative assemblies, and not the assemblies for parliamentary law. This is well expressed by a distinquished English writer on parliamentary law: "The great purpose of all rules and forms is to subserve the will of the assembly rather than to restrain it; to facilitate, and not to obstruct, the expression of their deliberative sense."

Additional Duties of the President of a Society, and the Vice Presidents. In addition to his or her duties as presiding officer, in many societies the president has duties as an administrative or executive officer. Where this is desired, the by-laws should clearly set forth these duties. They are outside of his or her duties as presiding officer of the assembly, and do not come within the scope of parliamentary law.

The same is true of vice presidents who are assigned varying areas of responsibility. They should be chosen with those duties in mind that are prescribed in the by-laws. It must be remembered that the first vice president must preside in the president's absence. In the cases of the president's illness, resignation, or death, the first vice president is the first in line to assume the presidency for the unexpired term, unless the rules otherwise specify how the vacancies should be filled. It is a mistake to elect a vice president who is not competent to perform the duties of president.

Hints to Inexperienced Presiding Officers. While in the chair, keep at hand your *constitution, by-laws,* and *rules of order.* These should be studied until you are perfectly familiar with them. You cannot tell when you may need this knowledge. If a member asks what motion to make in order to attain a certain object, you should be able to tell him or her at once **[10]**. You should memorize the list of ordinary motions arranged in their order of precedence, and should be able to refer to the *Table of Rules* so quickly that there will be no delay in deciding all points contained in them. Study the first ten sections of these Rules. They are simple, and will enable you to master parliamentary law more quickly. Read carefully sections **69-71**. This will familiarize you with the ordinary methods of conducting business in deliberative assemblies. Be aware that there are often different correct ways of doing the same thing, from which you can chose that which best fits the particular situation. You should know all the business that is to come regularly before the meeting, and call for it in its regular order. Keep at hand a list of the members of all committees, to guide you in nominating new committees.

When a motion is made, do not recognize any member or allow anyone to speak until the motion is seconded and you have stated the question. If there is no second and no response to your call for one, wait until you have announced that fact before you recognize another member, except when, before a main motion is seconded or stated, someone rises and says he or she rises ***(a) to move a reconsideration, (b) to call up the motion to reconsider,*** or ***(c) to move to take a question from the table.*** In any of these cases, the interrupting member is entitled to the floor **[3]** and should be recognized. If you make a mistake and assign the floor to the wrong person or recognize a motion that is out of order, correct the error as soon as your attention is called to it. After a vote is taken, before recognizing any member who addresses the chair, announce the result and also what question, if any, is then pending. Never wait for a merely routine motion to be seconded when you know no one objects to it. [See **8.**]

If a member ignorantly makes an improper motion, do not rule it out of order, but courteously suggest the proper one. If it is moved **"to lay the question on the table until 3 P.M."** because the form of the motion is incorrect, ask if the intention is **"to postpone the question to 3 P.M."** If the answer is yes, then state that the question is on the postponement to that time. If it is moved simply **"to postpone the question,"** without stating the time, do not rule it out of order, but ask the mover if he or she wishes **"to postpone the question indefinitely"** (which kills it) or **"to lay it on the table"** (which enables it to be taken up at any other time). You may then state the question in accordance with the motion he or she intended to make. If after a report has been presented and read, a member moves that **"it be received,"** ask the member if he or she means to move **"its adoption"** (or **"acceptance,"** which is the same thing), as the report has been already received. Unless someone objects to the reception of a report, no vote is taken on receiving it. This merely brings the report before the assembly and allows it to be read.

The chair of a committee usually has the most to say in reference to questions before the committee. The chair of an ordinary deliberative assembly, however, especially a large one, should, of all the members, have the least to say on the merits of pending questions. Simply because you know more about a matter than they do, never interrupt members when they are speaking. Never become excited. Never be unjust, even to the most troublesome member, or take advantage of a member's ignorance of parliamentary law, even when this is temporarily expedient. Know parliamentary law, but do make a display of your knowledge. Never be technical, or stricter than is absolutely necessary for the good of the meeting. Use your judgment. The assembly may be of such a nature (through its size, its lack of practice in parliamentary proceedures, and its good disposition) that a strict enforcement of the rules would impede rather than facilitate the conduct of business. In large assemblies, however, where there is a large volume of work to do, and especially in those where there is any likelihood of contention, strictly observing the rules is the only safe course.

59. Secretary or Clerk. The recording officer is called Clerk, Secretary, Recording Secretary (where there is also a Corresponding Secretary), or sometimes Recorder or Scribe. The secretary is the recording officer of the assembly and the guardian of all of its records except those that are specifically assigned to others, such as the treasurer's books. These records are open to inspection by any member at reasonable times. When a committee needs any records for the proper performance of its duties, they should be turned over to its chair. The same principle applies in boards and committees, whose records are accessible to members of the board or committee but to no others.

In addition to keeping the records of the society and the minutes of the meetings, it is the secretary's duty to: ***(a)*** *keep a register, or roll, of the members and to call the roll when required;* ***(b)*** *notify officers, committees, and delegates of their appointment, and to furnish com-*

mittees with all papers referred to them, and delegates with credentials; and **(c)** *sign with the president all orders on the treasurer authorized by the society, unless otherwise specified in the by-laws.* The secretary should also keep a book in which the constitution, by-laws, rules of order, and standing rules should all be written, leaving every other page blank. Whenever an amendment is made to any of them, in addition to being recorded in the minutes, it should be immediately entered on the page opposite to the article amended, with a reference in red ink to the date and page of the minutes where it is recorded.

In addition to the duties noted above, when there is only one secretary, it is the secretary's duty to send out proper notices of all called meetings, and of other meetings when necessary, and to conduct the correspondence of the society, except as otherwise provided. These duties, as well as any other responsibilities that the by-laws assign, fall to the ***Corresponding Secretary*** when there is one. If there is more than one secretary, the word secretary always refers to the recording secretary.

Before each meeting, the secretary makes out an ***order of business*** **[65]** for the chair's use. This shows in its exact order what business is to come before the assembly. The secretary should also have at each meeting a list of all standing committees, and such special committees as are in existence at the time, as well as the by-laws of the organization and its minutes. The secretary's desk should be near that of the chair. In the absence of the chair (if no vice president is present), it is the secretary's duty to call the meeting to order when the hour for opening the session arrives, and to preside until the election of a chair *pro tem.*, which should take place immediately. The secretary keeps a record of the proceedings, stating what was done and not what was said, unless it is to be published, and never making criticisms, favorable or otherwise, on anything said or done. The method of keeping this record, usually called the ***minutes,*** is explained below in **60**. When a committee is appointed, the secretary should hand the names of the committee, and all papers referred to it, to the chair of the committee, or another among its members. He or she should endorse on the reports of committees the date of their reception and what further action was taken on them, and preserve them among the records for which he or she is responsible. It is unnecessary to vote that a report be ***placed on file.*** This should be done without a vote, except in organizations that as a rule keep no records except their minutes and papers ordered on file.

60. The Minutes. The record of the proceedings of a deliberative assembly is usually called the ***Minutes,*** the ***Record,*** or the ***Journal.*** The essentials of this record are as follows: ***(a)*** *the kind of meeting,* ***regular*** (or ***stated***) or ***special,*** or ***adjourned regular*** or

adjourned special; **(b)** *name of the assembly;* **(c)** *date of meeting and place,* when it is not always the same; **(d)** *the fact of the presence of the regular chair and secretary,* or in their absence the names of their substitutes; **(e)** *whether the minutes of the previous meeting were approved, or their reading dispensed with,* the dates of the meetings being given when it is customary occasionally to transact business at other than the regular business meetings; **(f)** *all the main motions* (except those that were withdrawn) and *points of order* and *appeals, whether sustained or lost,* and *all other motions that were not lost or withdrawn;* and **(g)** *usually the hours of meeting and adjournment,* when the meeting is solely for business. The name of the member who introduced a main motion is usually recorded, but not that of the seconder.

In some societies the minutes are signed by both the president and the secretary. Whenever published, they should always be signed by both officers. If minutes are not habitually approved at the next meeting, then there should be written at the end of the minutes the word ***Approved*** and the date of the approval, which should be signed by the secretary. They should be entered in good black ink in a well-bound record book.[2]

The *Form* of the *Minutes* may be as follows:

At a regular meeting of the B.L. Society, held in their hall, on Sunday evening, March

15, 1992, the president in the chair, and Mr. K acting as secretary, the minutes of the previous meetings were read and approved. The Committee on Applications reported the names of Messrs. T and D as applicants for membership, and on motion of Ms. C they were admitted as members. The committee on .... reported through Mrs. G a series of resolutions, which were thoroughly discussed and amended, and finally adopted, as follows:

> ***Resolved, That* ....**
>
> **...**
>
> ***On the motion of Mr. L the society adjourned at 10 P.M.***
>
> **J. . . . K. . . .**

Secretary. In keeping the minutes much depends on the kind of meeting, and whether the minutes are to be published. In the meetings of ordinary societies and of boards of managers and trustees, there is no reason to report debates. In such cases, the principal duty of the secretary is to record what is ***done*** by the assembly, not what is said by the members. He or she should enter the essentials of a record, as stated above. When a count has been ordered or the vote is by ballot, he or she should enter the number of votes on each side. When the voting is by yeas and nays he or she should enter a list of those voting on each side. The proceedings of the ***committee of the whole,*** or while acting ***as if in committee of the whole,*** should not be entered in the minutes, but the report of the committee should be entered. When a question is considered informally, the proceedings should be kept as usual, because the only informality is in the debate. If a report containing resolutions has been agreed to, the resolutions should be entered in full as finally adopted by the assembly, thus: ***"The committee on . . . submitted a report with a series of resolutions that, after discussion and amendment, were adopted as follows: . . . "*** The resolutions as adopted should then be entered. When the proceedings are published, the procedure described below should be followed. If the report is of great importance the assembly should order it to be ***entered on the minutes.*** In this case, the secretary copies it in full upon the record.

When the regular meetings are held weekly, monthly, or quarterly, the minutes are read at the opening of each day's meeting. After correction, they are approved. When the meetings are held several days in succession with recesses during the day, the minutes are read at the opening of business each day. If the next meeting of the organization will not be held for a long period, as six months or a year, the minutes that have not been read previously should be read and approved before final adjournment. If this is not practical, the executive committee, or a special committee, should be authorized to correct and approve them. In this case the record should be signed and approved as usual. After the signatures the word ***Approved*** should be written with the date and the signature of the chair of the committee authorized to approve them. At the next meeting, six months or a year later, they need only be read when information is desired. It is too late to correct them intelligently. After the reading of the minutes is dispensed with, they can be taken up whenever nothing is pending. If not taken up previously, they come before the assembly at the next meeting before the reading of the later minutes. With this exception the motion to dispense with reading the minutes is essentially the equivalent of the motion to lay the minutes on the table. It is undebatable and requires only a majority vote. The minutes of a secret meeting, as for the trial of a member, should not be read at an open meeting. No part of the record that contains details of the trial should be made public.

Minutes to be Published. If the minutes are to be published, in addition to a strict record of what is done [described above], they should contain a list of the speakers on each side of every question, with an abstract of every speech (the speeches in full when written copies are furnished). The secretary should have assistance for this. When annual conventions wish to publish their proceedings in full, a stenographer must be employed to assist the secretary. Committee reports should be printed exactly as submitted, the minutes showing what action was taken by the assembly in regard to them. These may be printed with all additions in italics and parts struck out enclosed in brackets (a note explaining this prefixed to the report or resolutions). The reader thus can see both exactly what the committee reported and exactly what the assembly adopted or endorsed.

61. Executive Secretary. This officer is usually salaried in order to give all his or her time over to the work as executive officer or general manager of an organization under a board of managers and an executive committee **[50]**. This officer is called ***Corresponding Secretary*** in some organizations, but, unless the by-laws state otherwise, the title of corresponding secretary carries with it no duty other than conducting the correspondence of the society as explained in **59**. The office of the executive secretary is usually the organization's only office. The ***Executive Committee*** meets there to transact its business. The board of managers in such cases is usually large and so scattered as rarely to have regular meetings more often than quarterly. If the organization is a national one, it usually meets just before the annual convention to hear and act upon the annual report (prepared beforehand by the executive secretary and adopted by the executive committee). Immediately after the convention, the new board meets and organizes, electing an executive committee and an executive secretary when so authorized by the by-laws, and deciding upon the general policy for the year, leaving the details to the executive committee and the executive secretary. The board rarely meets more often than once or twice in addition to the meetings in connection with the annual meeting. Special meetings, however, are called when needed, as provided by its by-laws. In some organizations the executive secretary is elected by the convention. He or she is usually ex-officio secretary of the executive committee. The members of the executive committee giving their time gratuitously, it is the duty of the executive secretary to prepare for the committee all business that has not been assigned to others, and to see that all its instructions are carried out. He or she is expected to recommend work plans, and to conduct business in general under the executive committee, preparing the annual report that, after its adoption by the executive committee, should be adopted by the board, whose report it is, and then be submitted to the convention.

62. Treasurer. The duties of this officer vary in different societies. He or she usually acts as a banker, holding the funds deposited with him or her and paying them out on the order of the society signed by the president and the secretary. The treasurer is always required to make an annual report. In many societies the treasurer also provides a quarterly report, which may be in the form given below. If the society has auditors, this report should be submitted to them, with vouchers, in time to be audited before the meeting. After the auditors certify its accuracy and submit their report, the chair puts the question on adopting it. This has the effect of approving the treasurer's report, relieving him from responsibility in case of loss of vouchers, except in case of fraud. If there are no auditors the report when made should be referred to an auditing committee, who should report on it later.

It should always be remembered that the financial report is made for the information of members. Details of dates and separate payments for the same object uselessly impede its being understood. It is the auditing committee's duty to examine the details to see if the report is accurate. The best form for these financial reports depends on the nature of the society, and is best determined by examining those made in similar societies. The following brief report is in a form adapted to many societies where the financial work is a minor aspect of their activity.

REPORT OF THE TREASURER OF THE R. R. SOCIETY
FOR THE QUARTER ENDING MARCH 31, 1992

Receipts.

Balance on hand January 1, 1992 ...		$ 249.76
Initiation fees	$ 500.00	
Members' dues	1650.00	
Fines	100.00	2250.00
Total		$2499.76

Disbursements.

Rent of Hall	$ 500.00	
Electric lights	116.37	
Stationery and Printing	674.32	
Telephone and Fax	231.73	
Catering	350.00	
Staff Support	239.60	$2112.02
Balance on hand March 31, 1992 .		387.74
Total		$2499.76

C . . . . . . S . . . . . . ,
Treasurer.

Examined and found correct.

J . . . L. . . . ,
J . . . K. . . . , Auditing Committee.

Article XI: Miscellaneous

63. Session. A session of an assembly is virtually ***one meeting***. It may last for several days (as a ***session*** of a convention) or even months (as a ***session*** of Congress). It ends by an adjournment ***sine die*** (without day). Intermediate daily adjournments or recesses taken during the day do not break the continuity of the meetings which in reality constitute one session. Any meeting that is not an adjournment of another meeting begins a new session. In permanent societies whose by-laws provide for regular meetings every week, month, or year, for example, each meeting constitutes a separate session of the society. Any session can be prolonged by adjourning to another day.

In this manual the term ***meeting*** denotes *an assem-*

bling of the members of a deliberative assembly for any length of time, during which there is no separation of the members except for brief recess, as the morning, afternoon, and evening meetings of a convention whose session lasts for days. A ***meeting*** of an assembly is terminated by a temporary adjournment or a recess for a meal, etc.; a ***session*** of an assembly ends with an adjournment without day, and may consist of many meetings. An adjournment to meet again at some other time, even the same day, unless it is for only a few minutes, terminates the meeting, but not the session. The session includes all the adjourned meetings. The next meeting, in this case, would be an adjourned meeting of the same session.

In ordinary practice a meeting is closed by moving simply to ***adjourn.*** Either the rules or a resolution of the society set the time for the society's next meeting. If the society does not meet until the time for the next regular meeting as provided in the by-laws, then the adjournment closes the session, and is in effect an adjournment without day. When, however, the society establishes beforehand the time for the next meeting (either by a direct vote or by adopting a program for several meetings or even several days), the adjournment is in effect to a certain time and closes the meeting but not the session.

In such common expressions as ***quarterly meeting*** and ***annual meeting***, the word ***meeting*** denotes parliamentary ***session***, and covers all the adjourned meetings. Business that legally must be done at the ***annual meeting*** is done during the ***session*** that begins at the time specified for the annual meeting, though the session, by repeated adjournments, may last for days. If desired, the business may be postponed to the next regular meeting. Under *Renewal of Motions* **[38]** it is explained what motions can be repeated during the same session, and also the circumstances under which certain motions cannot be renewed until after the close of the next succeeding session.

A rule or resolution of a permanent nature may be adopted by a majority vote at any session of a society. It continues in force until it is rescinded. Such a standing rule does not materially interfere with the rights of a future session. Its affect on any future session may be suspended by majority vote. Rules may also be rescinded by majority vote, if notice of the proposed action is given at a previous meeting, or in the notice of the meeting. Rules may be rescinded without notice by a majority of the entire membership or by a two-thirds vote. To have greater stability, a rule must be placed in the constitutuion, by-laws, or rules of order. These are guarded by requiring notice of amendments and at least a two-thirds vote for their adoption. They are not subject to sudden changes and generally express the deliberate views of the entire society rather than the opinions or wishes of any particular meeting.

If the presiding officer becomes ill, the assembly

cannot elect a chair *pro tem.* to hold office beyond the session unless notice of the election is given at the previous meeting or in the call for the current meeting. It is improper for an assembly to postpone anything to a day beyond the next succeeding session, thus attempting to prevent the next session from considering the question. On the other hand, it is not permitted to move the reconsideration of a vote taken at a previous session. The motion to reconsider can be called up only if it is made during the previous session in a society having meetings as often as quarterly. Committees can be appointed to report to a future session.

64. Quorum. A quorum of an assembly is the number of members who must be present in order to transact business legally. The quorum refers to the number present, not to the number voting. The quorum of a mass meeting is the number present at the time. The quorum of a body of delegates, unless the by-laws provide for a smaller quorum, is a majority of the number enrolled as attending the convention, not the number of those appointed. The quorum of any deliberative assembly with an enrolled membership (unless the by-laws provide for a smaller quorum) is a majority of all the members. In societies where there are no annual dues and where membership is for life, the register of members is often unreliable as a list of the society's *bona fide* membership. In many such societies the presence of a majority of enrolled members at a business meeting is impossible. When such societies have no by-law establishing a quorum, the quorum consists of those who attend the meeting, provided that it is either a stated meeting or one that has been properly called.

In all ordinary societies the by-laws should provide for a quorum as large as can be depended upon to be present at all meetings, except under rare circumstances. In such an assembly the chair should not take the chair until a quorum is present, or until it is clear that no quorum will form. The only business that can be transacted in the absence of a quorum is ***(a)** the taking of measures to obtain a quorum,* ***(b)** fixing the time to which to adjourn,* and ***(c)** to adjourn,* or *to take a recess.* Unanimous consent cannot be given when a quorum is not present, and a notice given then is not valid. In the case of an annual meeting, where certain business for the year, as the election of officers, must be attended to during the session, the meeting should fix a time for an adjourned meeting and then adjourn. When an assembly has the power to compel the attendance of its members, if a quorum is not present at the appointed hour, the chair should wait a few minutes before taking the chair. In the absence of a quorum such an assembly may order a ***call of the house*** **[41]** and thus compel attendance of absentees, or it may adjourn, providing for an adjourned meeting if it pleases.

In committee of the whole, the quorum is the same as in the assembly. If it finds itself without a quorum, it can only rise and report to the assembly, which then adjourns. In any other committee the majority is a quorum, unless the assembly orders otherwise, and it must wait for a quorum before proceeding to business. Boards of trustees, managers, directors, etc., are on the same footing as committees as regards a quorum. Their power is delegated to them as a body. Unless so provided in the by-laws, they cannot independently determine their quorum (i.e., how many members must be present in order to act as a board or committee).

While no question can be decided in the absence of a quorum excepting those mentioned above, a member cannot interrupt another member while he or she is speaking in order to make the point of no quorum. The debate may continue in the absence of a quorum until someone raises the point while no one is speaking.

Although a quorum is competent to transact any business, it is usually unproductive to transact important business unless there is a fair attendance at the meeting or previous notice of such action has been given.

Care should be taken in amending the rule providing for a quorum. If the rule is struck out first, then the quorum instantly becomes a majority of all the members. In many societies it then becomes almost impossible to secure a quorum to adopt a new rule. The proper procedure is to amend by striking out certain words (or the whole rule) and inserting certain other words (or the new rule). This is made and voted on as one question.

65. Order of Business. It is customary for every permanent society to adopt an order of business for its meetings. When no rule has been adopted, the following is in order: **(a)** *Reading the Minutes of the previous meeting (and their approval);* **(b)** *Reports of Boards and Standing Committees;* **(c)** *Reports of Special (Select) Committees;* **(d)** *Special Orders;* **(e)** *Unfinished Business and General Orders;* and **(f)** *New Business.*

The minutes are read only once a day at the beginning of the day's business. The second item includes the reports of all Boards of Managers, Trustees, etc., as well as reports of such officers as are required to make them. The fifth item first includes the business pending and undisposed of at the previous adjournment, then the general orders that were on the calendar for the previous meeting and were not disposed of, and finally undisposed of matters postponed to the current meeting.

The secretary should always provide for the chair's use a memorandum of the order of business. This should show everything to come before the meeting. As soon as one matter is disposed of, the chair announces the next business in order. When reports are in order, he or she calls for the different reports in their order. When unfinished business is in order, the chair announces the different questions in their proper order, as indicated above. The chair thus always maintains control of business.

If it is desired to transact business out of its order, the rules must be suspended by a two-thirds vote [**22**]. Alternatively, as each resolution or report comes up, a majority can immediately lay it on the table, thus reaching any question that it desires first to dispose of. It is improper to lay on the table or to postpone a *class* of questions such as committee reports, or in fact anything but the question before the assembly.

66. Nominations and Elections. One or more candidates are usually nominated to fill an office before proceeding to an election. Nomination is unnecessary when the election is by ballot or roll call. Each member may then vote for any eligible person whether nominated or not. When the vote is *viva voce* or by rising, the nomination is like a motion to fill a blank. The different names are repeated by the chair as they are nominated. A vote is then taken on each name in the order of its nomination until one is elected. Nominations do not need to be seconded. Sometimes a nominating ballot is taken to determine the preferences of the members. In the election of the officers of a society, however, the usual practice is to have a committee make the nominations. When the committee makes its report, which consists of a ticket, the chair asks if there are any other nominations. These may then be made from the floor. The committee's nominations are treated just as if made by members from the floor. No vote is taken on accepting them.

When nominations are completed, the assembly proceeds to the election. Unless the by-laws prescribe otherwise, the voting is by any of the methods described under *Voting* **[46]**. Permanent societies usually vote by ballot, the balloting being continued until all offices are filled. An election takes effect immediately if the candidate is present and does not decline, or in his or her absence if he or she has consented to be a candidate. When a candidate who has not agreed to candidacy is absent, the election takes effect when he or she is notified of it, provided he or she does not decline immediately. It is too late to reconsider the vote on the election after the election has taken effect and the officer or member has learned of the fact. Unless the rules specify the time, an officer-elect takes office immediately. In most societies this time must be clearly designated.

67. Constitutions, By-laws, Rules of Order, and Standing Rules. The rules of a society may usually be conveniently divided into these four classes. In some societies, however, all the rules are found under one of these heads, and are called either the ***constitution,*** or the ***by-laws,*** or the ***standing rules.***

Provisions in regard to the constitution, etc., that are of a temporary nature should not be placed in the constitution, etc. They should be included in the motion to adopt, thus: "I move the adoption of the constitution reported by the committee and that the four directors receiving the most votes shall serve for three years, the four receiving the next largest number shall serve for two years, and the next four for one year, and that where there is a tie the classification shall be by lot;" or, "I move the adoption, etc . . . and that Article III shall not go into affect until after the close of this annual meeting." When the motion to adopt has been made, it may be amended to accomplish the object desired.

Constitutions. An incorporated society frequently has no constitution, a charter taking its place. Many other societies prefer to combine under one head the rules that are more commonly placed under the separate heads of constitution and by-laws. This is only objectionable when the by-laws are elaborate. It is then better to separate the most important rules and place them in the constitution. The constitution should contain only the following articles: *(1) Name and object of the society; (2) Qualification of members; (3) Officers and their election; (4) Meetings of the society* (including only what is essential, leaving details to the by-laws); *(5) How to amend the constitution.*

The first article may be divided into two, in which case there would be six articles. Usually some of the articles should be divided into sections. Nothing should be placed in the constitution that may be suspended, except the requiring of elections of officers by ballot. This may be qualified to allow the ballot to be dispensed with by unanimous vote when there is only one candidate for an office. The officers and board of managers or directors of an organization that meets only annually in convention, with the chairs of committees the organization has authorized and has required to report to the convention, should be *ex-officio* members of the convention if they are present at it. Provision for this should be made in the constitution. The constitution should require previous notice of an amendment and also a two-thirds or three-fourths vote for its adoption. When meetings are frequent, the making of a constitutional amendment should only be allowed at a quarterly or annual meeting, after having been proposed at the previous quarterly meeting. [See *Amendments to Constitutions, etc.,* **68.**]

By-laws, except those placed in the constitution and the rules of order, should include all rules of such importance that they cannot be changed in any way without previous notice. Few societies adopt any special rules of order of their own, contenting themselves with putting a few such rules in their by-laws and then adopting some standard work on parliamentary law as their authority. When a society is incorporated, the charter may take the place of the constitution. The by-laws then contain all the rules of the society, except those in the charter that cannot be changed without previous notice. The by-laws should always provide for their amendment as shown in **68,** and also for a quorum, **64.** The suspension of any by-law, if it is desired to permit this, should be specifically provided for. By-laws, except those relating to business procedure, can only be suspended when they expressly provide for their suspension. By-laws in the nature of rules of order may be suspended by a two-thirds vote [see **22**].

By-laws should define the duties of the presiding and recording officers of a deliberative assembly [**58–59**]. If a society wishes to provide for honorary officers or members, it is well to do so in the by-laws. Unless the by-laws state otherwise, these positions are strictly complimentary. They carry with them the right to attend meetings and to speak, but not to make motions or to vote. Honorary presidents and vice presidents should sit on the platform. They do not, however, preside by virtue of their honorary office. An honorary office is not strictly an office. It in no way disbars a member from holding a real office or being assigned any duty. Like a college honorary degree, it is perpetual unless rescinded. It is proper, when desired, to include in the published list of honorary officers the names of all upon whom the honor has been conferred, even though deceased.

Rules of Order should contain rules relating only to the orderly transaction of business in meetings and to the duties of officers. Most of these rules should be as uniform as possible for all ordinary societies. There is great advantage in following a standard procedure. Societies should adopt some generally accepted rules of order or parliamentary manual as their authority, and then adopt only those special rules of order that are needed to supplement it. Every society, in its by-laws or rules of order, should adopt a rule such as this: "The rules contained in [specifying the work on parliamentary practice] shall govern the society in all cases to which they are applicable, and in which they are not inconsistent with the by-laws or the special rules of order of this society." Without such a rule, anyone so inclined can cause great trouble in a meeting.

Standing Rules should contain only rules that may be adopted without prior notice by a majority vote at any business meeting. A vote on their adoption or amendment may be reconsidered before or after adoption. They may be suspended by a majority vote at any meeting, or may be amended or rescinded by a two-thirds vote. They may be amended or rescinded by a majority vote if notice of the proposed action is given at a previous meeting or in the call for the current meeting. Because a majority may suspend any standing rule at any meeting, these rules do not compromise the freedom of any meeting. Their adoption therefore requires no notice. They are generally adopted as needed rather than at the organization of a society. The by-laws of a society are sometimes called standing rules. It is better, however, to follow the usual classification of rules as given in this section. The following is an example of a standing rule: ***Resolved, That the meetings of this society from April 1 to September 30 shall begin at 7:30 P.M., and during the rest of the year at 8 P.M.***

No standing rule, resolution, or motion is in order that conflicts with the constitution, by-laws, rules of order, or standing rules.

68. Amendments of Constitutions, By-laws, and Rules of Order. Constitutions, by-laws, and rules of order that have been adopted, and contain no rule for their amendment, may be amended at any regular business meeting by a vote of the majority of the entire membership. If the amendment is submitted in writing at the previous regular business meeting, they may be amended by a two-thirds vote of those voting, a quorum being present. However, each society should adopt rules for the amendment of its constitution, by-laws, and rules of order, adapted to its own needs, but always requiring previous notice and a two-thirds vote. When assemblies meet regularly only once a year, the constitution, etc., should provide that copies of the amendment be sent with the notices to the members or the constituency, instead of requiring that amendments be submitted at the previous annual meeting. The requirements may vary to suit the needs of each assembly, but ample notice should always be provided to the members or the constituency.

In societies having frequent meetings, as well as monthly or quarterly meetings more specifically devoted to business, it is well to allow amendments to the by-laws, etc. to be adopted only at the quarterly or annual meetings. In specifying when an amendment must be submitted, "*the* previous regular meeting" should be used instead of "*a* previous regular meeting." In the latter case, action on the amendment might be delayed indefinitely to suit the mover, thus defeating the purpose of giving notice. In prescribing the vote necessary for the adoption of an amendment, the expression **"a vote of two-thirds of the members"** should never be used in ordinary societies, especially in large organizations with quorums smaller than a majority of the membership. In such societies, two-thirds of the membership (i.e., two-thirds of the entire membership) is rarely present at a meeting. If it is desired to require a larger vote than two-thirds (i.e., two-thirds of the votes cast, a quorum being present), the expression "a vote of two-thirds of the members present," should be used. Notice of the amendment may be given orally when not required to be submitted in writing. In any case, unless the rule requires that the amendment itself be submitted, only its purport is necessary.

When the by-laws require only previous notice of an amendment, if a committee is appointed to revise the by-laws and report at a certain meeting, this is the only notice required, and the amendment can be acted upon immediately. When the by-laws require the amendment or **"notice of such amendment"** to be submitted at the previous regular meeting, the amendment cannot be taken up until the meeting following the meeting at which the committee submits its report. Because a substitute is an amendment, the committee may submit a substitute for the by-laws unless the nature of its report is prescribed. Great care should be taken to comply with every rule in regard to the amendment of constitutions, etc.

An amendment to the constitution, or anything else that is adopted, goes into effect immediately upon its adoption, unless the motion to adopt specifies another time for this, or the assembly previously adopts a motion that specifies a time. While the amendment is pending, a motion may be made to amend by adding a ***proviso*** similar to this, "Provided, that this does not go into effect until after the close of this annual meeting." Alternatively, while an amendment is pending, an incidental motion may be adopted that the amendment shall not take effect until a specified time if it is adopted. This requires only a majority vote.

Amending a proposed amendment to the constitution, etc. Subject to certain restrictions, a ***proposed amendment*** to the constitution, etc., may be amended without notice by a majority vote. The assembly is not limited to adopting or rejecting the amendment exactly as it is proposed. No amendment is in order, however, that *increases* the modification of the rule to be amended. Otherwise, advantage could be taken of this by submitting a very slight change that would not attract attention and then moving the serious modification as an amendment to the amendment.

For example, if the by-laws placed the annual dues of members at $30.00, and an amendment is pending to strike out 3 and insert 6, an amendment would be in order to change the 3 to any number between 3 and 6; but an amendment would not be in order that changed the 3 to any number greater than 6 or less than 3. Had notice been given that it was proposed to increase the dues to more than $60.00, or the reduce them below $30.00, members might have been present to oppose the change, who did not attend because they were not opposed to an increase as high as $60.00.

The same principle applies to an amendment in the form of a substitute. The proposed substitute is open to amendments that diminish the changes, but not to amendments that increase those that are proposed, or introduce new changes. Thus, if an amendment is pending that substitutes a new rule for one that prescribes the initiation fee and annual dues, and the substitute does not change the annual dues, then a motion to amend it that changes the annual dues is out of order. The notice must be sufficiently definite to give fair warning to all parties interested as to the exact points that are to be modified. The proposed amendment is a main motion, and that is the only question before the assembly. Like other main motions, it is subject to amendments of the first and second degree, and no amendment that is not germane to it is in order.

A society can amend its constitution and by-laws in order to change the compensations and duties of officers already elected, or even to eliminate an office. If it is desired that the amendment should not affect officers already elected, a motion to that effect should be adopted before voting on the amendment. Alternatively, a proviso can be added to the motion to amend, stating that the amendment should not affect officers already elected. There is something in the nature of a contract between a society and its officers that either one can modify to some extent, or even terminate, but this must be done with reasonable consideration for the other party. A secretary, for instance, has no right to refuse to perform his or her duties on the grounds that he or she has handed in his or her resignation. On the other hand, the society cannot compel the secretary to continue in office beyond a reasonable time to allow for choosing his or her successor.

Care should be exercised in wording the sections providing for amending the constitution, etc., to avoid such tautology as "amend, or add to, or repeal," or "alter or amend," or "amend or in any way change." The one word *amend* covers any change whatever in the constitution, etc., whether it is a word or a paragraph that is added or struck out, or replaced by another word or paragraph, or whether a new constitution, etc., is submitted for the old one.

PART II:

Organization, Meetings, and Legal Rights of Assemblies

Article XII: Organization and Meetings

69. AN OCCASIONAL OR MASS MEETING
- *(a) Organization*
- *(b) Adoption of Resolutions*
- *(c) Committee to Draft Resolutions*
- *(d) Semi-Permanent Mass Meetings*

70. A PERMANENT SOCIETY
- *(a) First Meeting*
- *(b) Second Meeting*
- *(c) Regular Meetings of a Society*

71. MEETING OF A CONVENTION OR ASSEMBLY OF DELEGATES
- *(a) An Organized Convention*
- *(b) A Convention not yet Organized*

69. An Occasional or Mass Meeting. ***(69a) Organization***. Before calling a meeting of other than an organized society, the following ***Preliminary Steps*** should be taken: The persons calling the meeting should decide upon the time and place of the meeting, how notice of it is to be given, who will call the meeting to order, who is to be nominated as chair, and who is to explain the meeting's purpose. It is also often good policy to draft in advance a set of resolutions to submit to the meeting.

Mass meetings are usually called to order ten or fifteen minutes after the appointed time, when the one chosen for the purpose steps to the front and says, "The meeting will please come to order; I move that Ms. A act as [or I nominate Ms. A for] chair of this meeting." Someone else says, "I second the motion [or nomination]." The first member then puts the question to vote, saying, "It has been moved and seconded that Ms. A act as [or Ms. A has been nominated for] chair of this meeting; those in favor of the motion [or nomination] say aye." When the affirmative vote is taken, he or she says, "Those opposed say no." If the majority vote is in the affirmative, the member says, "The ayes have it, and Ms. A is elected chair. She will please take the chair." If the motion is lost the member announces the fact, calls for the nomination of someone else for chair, and proceeds with the new nomination as above.

Instead of making the motion to nominate, the member who calls the meeting to order may act as a temporary chair and say, "The meeting will please come to order; will someone nominate a chair?" He or she puts the question to vote on the nomination as described above. This can be dangerous in large meetings where an incompetent person may be nominated and elected as chair. In large assemblies, the member who nominates, with one other member, often conducts the elected presiding officer to the chair. The chair then makes a short speech of thanks to the assembly for the honor conferred on him or her.

When the presiding officer takes the chair, he or she says, "The first business in order is the election of a secretary." Someone then makes a motion as just described, or he or she says, "I nominate Mr. B." The chair then puts the question as below. Sometimes several names are called out. As the chair hears them, he or she says, "Mr. B. is nominated; Ms. C is nominated," etc. He or she then takes the vote on the first nominated, putting the question in this form: "As many as are in favor of Mr. B for secretary say aye; those opposed say no. The chair is in doubt: those in favor of Mr. B for secretary will rise; those opposed will rise. The negative has it and the motion is lost. As many as are in favor of Ms. C for secretary say aye; those opposed say no. The ayes have it, and Ms. C is elected secretary. She will please take her place at the desk." If Ms. C is not elected, the vote is taken on the next nominee and continues until someone is chosen. The secretary should take his or her seat near the chair, and keep a record of the proceedings as described in **59**. The chair should always stand in putting the question to vote. In large assemblies he or she should also stand when stating the question. During debate the chair should be seated and pay attention to the discussion. Nominations may be seconded, but this is often not required. They are usually not debated. However, the one making the nomination and the one seconding it sometimes say a few words at the time in favor of their nominee. A nomination cannot be amended. If additional officers are desired, they may be elected in the same manner as the secretary.

(69b) Adoption of Resolutions. The Presiding Officer (or Chair) and the secretary are usually the only officers necessary, so as soon as the secretary is elected, the chair directs him or her to read the call for the meeting. The chair then fully explains the purpose of the meeting or calls on the person most familiar with it to do so. Afterward, someone should immediately offer a series of resolutions prepared beforehand. Alternatively, someone makes a motion to appoint a committee to prepare resolutions upon the subject. In the first case he or she rises and says, "Mr./Madame Chair." The chair responds, "Ms. C." Ms. C, having thus obtained the floor, says, "I move the adoption of the following resolutions." She reads them and hands them to the chair. Someone else then says, "I second the motion." The chair then says, "It has been moved and seconded to adopt the following resolutions." He or she then reads the resolutions or directs the secretary to do so. When this is done, the chair says, "The question is on the adoption of the resolutions." If no one rises immediately, he or she asks, "Are you ready for the question?" The resolutions are now open to debate and amendment. They may be referred to a committee, or may have any other subsidiary motion applied to them. When the debate appears to be concluded, the chair again asks, "Are you ready for the question?" If no one then rises, he or she says, "As many as are in favor of the adoption of the resolutions say aye." After the ayes have voted, he or she says, "As many as are of a contrary opinion [or are opposed] say no." The chair then announces the result of the vote as follows: "The ayes have it [or the motion is carried] and the resolutions are adopted." If the debate has lasted any length of time, the chair should have the resolutions read again before he or she takes the vote.

In legislative assemblies, all resolutions, bills, etc., are sent to the clerk's desk. The title of the bill and the name of the member introducing it are endorsed on each. In such bodies, however, there are several clerks and only one chair. In most assemblies there is only one clerk or secretary. Because he or she has to keep the minutes, he or she should not be constantly interrupted to read every resolution offered. Unless there is a rule or established custom to the contrary, it is usually much better in such assemblies to hand all resolutions, reports, etc., directly to the chair. If they were read by the member introducing them and no one calls for another reading, the chair may omit repeating them when he or she thinks they are fully understood. [For the manner of reading and stating the question when the resolution contains several paragraphs, see **24**.]

Dividing Resolutions. Sometimes the committee reports several independent resolutions relating to different subjects. When this is the case, if a single member requests division, the chair must state the question separately on the resolution or resolutions relating to each subject. If the resolutions relate to a single subject but each can stand independently if all the rest are rejected, they may be divided by a majority vote on a motion to divide the question [**24**]. If the resolutions are so connected that they cannot stand alone, the correct way to secure a separate vote on any objectionable resolution is to move to strike it out. When the chair states the question on striking it out, the resolution is open to amendments of the second degree, in order to perfect it, before the vote is taken on striking it out [**33**].

Amending a Resolution. If it is desired to amend a pending resolution (i.e., a resolution that the chair has stated as before the assembly for action), a member rises and obtains the floor as already described. He or she offers, or moves, his or her amendment thus: "I move to insert the words 'with asphalt' after the word 'paved.'" If the motion is not seconded immediately, the chair asks if the motion is seconded. In a large assembly he or she should repeat the motion before making this inquiry, since members willing to second the motion may not have heard it. The chair must usually assume that some members do not hear what is said from the floor, and therefore that he or she must always repeat motions and the result of votes. When the motion is seconded, the chair states the question thus: "It is moved and seconded to amend the resolution by inserting the words 'with asphalt' after the word 'paved'. Are you ready for the question?" The question is now open to debate and amendment. This must be confined, however, to the amendment, because it then supersedes the resolution and becomes what is termed the *immediately pending question*. If no one rises to claim the floor, the chair puts the question thus, "As many as are in favor of the amendment [or motion] say aye; those opposed say no. The ayes have it and the amendment is adopted. The question is now on the resolution as amended, which is as follows [repeat the amended resolution]. Are you ready for the question?" The resolution is again open to debate and amendment, because it has again become the immediately pending question. When the chair thinks the debate ended, he or she asks, "Are you ready for the question?" If no one rises to claim the floor, he or she puts the question on the resolution thus: "The question is on adopting the following resolution: "Resolved, That . . . Those in favor of the motion [or of adopting the resolution] say aye; those opposed say no. The ayes have it, and the resolution is adopted."

(69c) Committee to Draft Resolutions. If it is preferred to appoint a committee to draft resolutions, a member, after he or she has addressed the chair and has been recognized, says, "I move that the chair appoint a committee of five to draft resolutions expressive of the sense of this meeting on," etc., adding the subject for which the meeting was called. When this is seconded, the chair states the question thus: "It has been moved and seconded that the chair appoint a committee of five to draft resolutions, etc. [repeat the motion]. Are you ready for the question?" If no one rises the chair may repeat the question thus: "As many as are in favor of the motion say aye; those opposed say no. The ayes have it and the motion is adopted." Or, it may be put thus: "The question is, 'Shall a committee of five be appointed by the chair to draft resolutions, etc. [repeat the motion]? As many as are of the affirmative will raise their right hands. As many as are of the negative will signify it in the same way. The affirmative has it and the motion is adopted. The chair will appoint Messrs. A, B, and C, Ms. D, and Mrs. E as the committee on resolutions. The committee will withdraw and prepare the resolutions as quickly as possible. What is the further pleasure of the meeting?"

In a mass meeting or in any large assembly, it is safer to have the chair appoint all committees. If the assembly prefers a different method, the procedure is as described in **32**. Alternatively, the following method may be adopted. A member moves that "a committee be appointed to draft resolutions," etc. When this motion is adopted, the chair asks, "Of how many shall the committee consist?" If only one number is suggested, he or she announces that the committee will consist of that number. If several numbers are suggested, the chair states them and then takes a vote on each, beginning with the largest, until a number is selected. He or she then asks, "How shall the committee be appointed?" This is usually decided without the formality of a vote. The chair may ***appoint*** the committee. In this case the chair names the committee and no vote is taken. Alternatively, the committee may be ***nominated*** by the chair, or by members of the assembly (no member naming more than one, except by unanimous consent). The assembly then votes on their appointment. When the chair nominates, after stating the names, he or she puts one question on the entire committee, "As many as are in favor of these members constituting the committee say aye," etc. If nominations are made by members of the assembly, and more names are mentioned than the number of the committee, a separate vote must be taken on each name, in the order of their nomination, until the committee is filled.

When the committee is appointed, it should at once retire and agree upon a report. This should be written out as described in **52**. During the committee's absence other business may be attended to, or the time may be occupied with hearing speeches. When the committee returns to the room, the chair should announce, as soon as the pending business is disposed of or the member speaking closes, that the assembly will now hear the report of the committee on resolutions. Before making this announcement, the chair may ask if the committee is prepared to report. If the chair fails to notice the return of the committee, the committee chair takes the first opportunity to obtain the floor, and says, "The committee appointed to draft resolutions is prepared to report." The chair tells him or her that the assembly will now hear the report. The committee chair then reads it, immediately moves its adoption, and hands it to the presiding officer. The committee is then dissolved without any action of the assembly. The chair then proceeds as when any resolutions are offered. If adoption of the resolutions is not immediately desired, they may be debated, modified, or their consideration postponed, etc., as explained in **10**.

When the business is done for which the assembly was convened, or when from any other cause it is desired to close the meeting, someone "moves to adjourn." If no time has been appointed for another meeting, this motion may be amended and debated as any other main motion. If the motion is carried, and no other time for meeting has been appointed, the chair, in case the ayes and noes are nearly equal, says, "The ayes seem to have it, the ayes have it, the motion is adopted, and we stand adjourned without day (*sine die*)." If the vote is overwhelmingly in the affirmative, the expression, "The ayes seem to have it," should be omitted. If a time for an adjourned meeting has been appointed, the chair declares the assembly "adjourned to 8 P.M. next Wednesday evening," or whatever the appointed time. Before declaring the adjournment, or even taking a vote on adjourning, the chair should be satisfied that all required notices are given.

(69d) Semi-Permanent Mass Meetings. It is sometimes desirable to continue the mass meetings until a certain goal is reached. In such cases the assembly may prefer first to form a temporary organization, and then form their semi-permanent organization with more deliberation. If so, the assembly is organized as just described, only adding ***pro tem.*** to the title of the officers, thus, ***chair pro tem.*** The ***pro tem.*** is never used to address the officers. As soon as the secretary ***pro tem***. is elected, a committee is usually appointed to nominate the semi-permanent officers, as in the case of a convention. A committee on rules should also be appointed. This committee should recommend a few rules providing for the time and place of meeting, for some authority on parliamentary law, and for the number and length of speeches allowed, if two speeches not to exceed ten minutes each is not satisfactory.

The presiding officer or chair is often called "President". Sometimes many honorary vice presidents are appointed. In large formal meetings the vice presidents sit on the platform beside the president. When he or she is absent or has to leave, the first vice president on the list who is present takes the chair.

70. A Permanent Society. ***(70a) First Meeting.*** Persons who wish to form a permanent society should consult together and carefully lay their plans before calling a meeting to organize the society. In calling the meeting, they should be careful to see to it that there is a majority in sympathy with their plans. If they neglect this and publish an invitation to all interested in the object to attend the meeting, those who originate the work may find themselves in the minority. They may not favor the constitution that is adopted and may not want to join the society after it is organized. Having taken all the preliminary steps, then, as described in **69**, they invite those whom they believe to be in sympathy with their general plans to meet at a certain time and place to consider the question of organizing a society for a certain purpose. One of the first steps should be to obtain copies of the constitutions and by-laws of similar societies for the use of the committee in drafting their own.

It is common practice in meetings called to organize a society, or in mass meetings, to begin ten or fifteen minutes after the appointed time. The person selected beforehand for the purpose steps forward and says,

"The meeting will please come to order; I move that Mr. A act as chair of this meeting." Someone "seconds the motion." The person who made the motion then puts it to vote (or, as it is called, ***puts the question***): [See *Mass Meeting*, **69**.] When the chair is elected, he or she takes the chair and announces the election of a secretary as the first business in order.

After the secretary is elected, the chair calls on the member who is most interested in forming the society to state the meeting's purpose. This member rises and says, "Mr./Madame Chair." The chair announces his or her name. The member then explains the purpose of the meeting. When the member has finished his or her remarks, the chair may call on other members to give their opinions on the subject. Sometimes members call out to hear a particular speaker. The chair should observe the wishes of the assembly and should avoid being too strict, but must not allow anyone to take too much time and weary the assembly.

When sufficient time has been spent informally, someone should offer a resolution to take definite action. If the meeting is to be large, those who initiate it should agree beforehand on what is to be done, and should be prepared to offer a suitable resolution at the appropriate time. The resolution can be in this form: "Resolved, That it is the sense of this meeting that a society for [state the object of the society] should now be formed in this city." After it is seconded and the chair states it, this resolution is open to debate and amendment, and is treated as described in **69**. This preliminary motion can be offered at the opening of the meeting. When the meeting is large, this is generally preferable to beginning with informal discussion.

After or even before this preliminary motion has been voted on, one like the following may be offered: "I move that the chair appoint a committee of five to draft a constitution and by-laws for a society for [here state the object], ***and that it report at an adjourned meeting of this assembly."*** This motion is debatable. It can be amended by striking out and adding words, etc.

After this committee is appointed, the chair may ask, "Is there any other business to be attended to?" or, "What is the further pleasure of the assembly [or club, or convention, etc.]?" When all business is concluded, a motion may be made to adjourn at a certain time and place. After this motion is seconded and the chair states it, it is open to debate and amendment. It is usually better to establish the time of the next meeting at an earlier stage of the current meeting, and when it is desired to close the current meeting to move simply "to adjourn." This motion cannot be amended or debated. When it is carried, the chair says, "This meeting stands adjourned to meet at . . .", etc., specifying the time and place of the next meeting.

(70b) Second Meeting. If the officers of the first meeting are present at the next one, they serve until the permanent officers are elected. When the hour arrives for the meeting, the chair stands and says, "The meeting will please come to order." As soon as the assembly is seated, he or she says, "The secretary will read the minutes of the last meeting." The chair then sits. Anyone who notices an error in the minutes should state the fact as soon as the secretary finishes reading them. If there is no objection, the chair, without waiting for a motion, directs the secretary to make the correction. The chair then says, "There being no [further] corrections, the minutes stand approved as read [or as corrected]."

The chair then announces as the next business in order the hearing of the report of the committee on the constitution and by-laws. The chair of the committee, after addressing the chair and gaining recognition, says, "The committee appointed to draft a constitution and by-laws has agreed upon the following resolutions, and has directed me to report the same and move their adoption." He or she then reads them, moves their adoption, and hands them to the chair. After the motion is seconded, the chair says, "It has been moved and seconded to adopt the constitution and by-laws reported by the committee. The question is on the adoption of the constitution, which will now be read." The constitution is then read from the platform by the secretary or the committee chair, as the chair directs. Because the constitution has already been read, this second reading may be dispensed with by general consent. The chair then reads (or has someone read) the first paragraph, and asks if there are any amendments proposed to this paragraph. When the assembly has amended it, the chair says, "There being no [further] amendments to this paragraph, the next will be read." No vote should be taken on adopting the separate paragraphs. The chair thus proceeds through the entire constitution, and then declares the entire constitution open to amendment. This is the time to insert additional paragraphs, or make any amendments to the earlier paragraphs rendered necessary by changes made in the later ones.

When the chair thinks the constitution has been modified to suit the wishes of the assembly, he or she asks, "Are you ready for the question?" If no one wishes to speak, the chair puts the question, "As many as are in favor of adopting the constitution as amended say aye;" and then, "As many as are opposed say no." The chair should clearly announce the result of the vote. This should never be omitted. Only a majority vote is required to adopt the constitution of a new society, or to amend it before it is adopted.

The chair now states that the constitution having been adopted, those wishing to become members must sign it (and pay the initiation fee, if required by the constitution). If the assembly is large, the chair suggests that a recess be taken for that purpose. A motion is then made to take a recess until the constitution is signed. Only those who sign the constitution join the society and are entered on the roll of members. While the payment of the initiation fee is strictly a prerequisite to the right to vote, it should be waived at this meeting for those who are unprepared to pay immediately.

When the recess expires, the chair calls the meeting to order and says, "The secretary will read the roll of members." This is necessary in order that all may know who are entitled to take part in future proceedings. After the roll has been read, the chair says, "The question before the assembly is on the adoption of the by-laws reported to the committee. The secretary will please read them." He or she then proceeds exactly as in the case of the constitution (described above). Because the motion to adopt the constitution and the by-laws reported by the committee was made when the committee made its report, no further motion is necessary.

When the by-laws are adopted, the chair says, "The next business in order is the election of the permanent officers of the society." The by-laws should prescribe the method of nomination and election of officers. This method should be followed strictly. If the by-laws do not prescribe the method of nomination, the chair asks, "How shall the officers be nominated?" Someone may immediately move that the chair appoint a committee to nominate the permanent officers of the society. When this motion is adopted, the chair appoints the committee, which retires and agrees upon a ticket. During the absence of the committee the assembly may transact any business it pleases, or it may take a recess.

When the committee returns to the hall, as soon as pending business is disposed of, the chair calls on the committee chair for the report. The committee chair reads the list of nominations, and hands it to the chair. The chair reads the list, and then asks, "Are there any further nominations?" Any member may now rise and address the chair to nominate anyone else for any office, or he or she may nominate one person for each office, thus proposing a new ticket. The chair announces the nominations as made. When the chair thinks that no more names will be proposed, he or she asks, "Are there any more nominations?" If there is no response, and the by-laws prescribe that the election shall be by ballot, as they usually should, the chair appoints tellers and directs them to distribute blank ballots upon which each member writes the name of each office and the person for whom he or she votes to fill that office. When the ballots are filled out, the chair directs the tellers to collect them. They may use any convenient receptacle for this purpose. To be sure that the tellers have not missed any members, the chair inquires if all have voted who wish to. When all who wish to vote have done so, the chair announces that "the polls are closed." The tellers then count the ballots. The first appointed teller reports the vote [see *Voting by Ballot*, **46**]. The chair then announces the election of all the candidates who received a majority vote. The temporary officers are immediately replaced by the permanent ones elected. If the president is elected on this first ballot he or she immediately takes the chair. If any office remains unfilled, the chair immediately orders the tellers to distribute blank ballots, and directs the assembly to prepare ballots for it. Balloting is continued until all offices are filled. Voting is not limited to the nominees. Every member is free to vote for any member who is not declared ineligible by the by-laws.

When all offices have been filled, the chair should mention any business that he or she knows requires immediate attention. Committees should probably be appointed for various purposes, as described in the by-laws, and the place of meeting should be determined. It is possible that an adjourned meeting may be necessary to complete the organization before beginning the regular work of the society. When work is completed, or when an adjourned meeting has been provided for and the lateness of the hour requires an adjournment, someone should move to adjourn. If the motion is carried, the chair announces the votes and declares the assembly adjourned. If there can be any question as to when and where the next meeting is to be held, the chair should announce the time and place.

If the society expects to own real estate, it should be incorporated according to the laws of the state in which it is situated. A member of the committee on the constitution should consult a lawyer on this matter, before this second meeting, to assure that the constitution conforms to the laws of the state. The trustees, or managers, or directors, are usually instructed to take the proper measures to have the society incorporated.

(70c) Regular Meetings of a Society. After a society is properly organized, its regular business meetings are conducted as follows. When the hour fixed for the meeting to begin arrives, the presiding officer takes the chair and calls the meeting to order. He or she then directs the secretary to read the minutes of the last meeting. When they are read, the chair asks, "Are there any corrections to the minutes?" If none are suggested, he or she adds, "There being none, the minutes stand approved as read." If any corrections are suggested, the secretary makes them, unless there is opposition. If there is difference of opinion, someone moves to amend the minutes, or the chair, without waiting for a motion, puts the question on the suggested amendment. When this has been settled, the chair asks, "Are there any further corrections [or amendments] to the minutes?" If not, the chair adds, "There being none, the minutes stand approved as corrected." The chair then announces the next business in order, following the order of business prescribed by the rules of the society.

If the order of business is the same as given in **65**, as soon as the minutes are read and approved, the chair says, "The next business in order is hearing the reports of the standing committees." The chair then calls on each committee in its order for its report, "Has the committee on applications for membership any report to make?" The committee reports as shown above, or one of its members answers that it has no report to make. When the chair knows that there are few if any committee reports, it is better, after making the announcement of the business, for the chair to ask, "Have these committees any reports to make?" After a short pause, if no one rises to report, the chair states, "There being no reports from the standing committees, the next business in order is hearing the reports of special committees." The chair then acts exactly as with standing committees. The chair should always have a list of the committees in order to call upon them, and as a guide for the appointment of new committees.

Having attended to the reports of committees, the chair announces the next business in order, and so on until the business of the meeting has been disposed of. Someone then moves to adjourn. If this motion is carried, the chair announces the vote and declares the assembly adjourned.

The meetings of different societies vary greatly and should be managed differently in order to obtain the best results. Some societies require a strict enforcement of parliamentary rules. Others obtain the best results with informal procedures. The presiding officer should proceed with tact and common sense, especially when working with an intelligent group.

71. Meeting of a Convention or Assembly of Delegates. ***(71a) An Organized Convention.*** If a convention is an organized body (i.e., when convened it has a constitution, by-laws, and officers), a credentials (or registration) committee and a program committee should be appointed before the meeting. These committees may be appointed at the previous convention by the executive board or the president, as the by-laws prescribe. The committee on credentials or registration should be on hand before the meeting in order to be prepared to submit its report immediately after the opening addresses. It should furnish each delegate when he or she registers with a badge or card as evidence of his or her being a delegate and having the right of admission to the hall. The program committee usually should have programs printed in advance. It is often better that the constituent bodies be furnished in advance with copies of the program. This should always be done when there is difficulty in getting full delegations to attend. In addition to these two committees, a number of local committees are usually appointed by the local society, as on entertainment, etc. One of the general officers usually performs the duty of a committee on transportation, to obtain reductions in air fares, etc.

When the hour appointed for the meeting arrives, the president, as the permanent presiding officer of a convention is usually called, stands at the desk and strikes it with the gavel to attract attention, saying, "The convention will come to order." There is usually a lot of confusion and noise at the opening of large conventions. Self-control, firmness, and tact are required of the presiding officer to preserve proper order so that all members may hear and be heard. The chair is mistaken when he or she tries to stop the noise by pounding with the gavel and shouts to be heard over the commotion on the floor. The chair does better to set the example of being quiet, and to stop all business when the noise is such that members cannot hear. Members should be required to be seated and to refrain from talking except when addressing the chair.

It is customary to have some opening exercises when the convention comes to order. The nature of these depends on the character of the convention. In the majority of cases the convention is opened with prayer, an address of welcome, and a response. The program is the president's guide to the order of business, even though the convention has not yet adopted it. It should provide for hearing the report of the credentials committee as soon as the opening exercises are concluded, so that it may be known who are entitled to vote. This committee's report usually consists merely of a list of the delegates and their alternates, if any, whose credentials have been found correct, and of the ex-officio members of the convention. No one is on the list who has not registered as present. The constitution should always provide that the officers of the convention, the members of the board of managers, and the chairs of the committees that are required to report at the convention, shall be ex-officio members of the convention if they are present.

When the report of the credentials committee is presented, it is read either by the chair of the committee or by the reading secretary, or official reader, if there is one. Neither this nor any other report should be read from the platform. When the chair of a committee cannot be heard, the report should be read by a reading secretary or official reader, who should be appointed in every large convention solely for the purpose of reading resolutions, reports, etc.

When two sets of delegates contest credentials and there is serious doubt as to which is entitled to recognition, the committee should omit both from the list and report the dispute. However, if the credentials committee thinks the contest unjustified, it should ignore it and enter on the list the names of the legitimate delegates. Neither of the contested delegations can vote on the motion to substitute one delegation for another, nor can a contested delegation vote on a motion to strike out the names of its delegates.

A motion should be made to accept or adopt the report of the credentials committee. After the chair states this motion, it is open to debate and amendment. All persons whose names are on the list of members as reported by the credentials committee and amended by the convention—and they alone—are entitled to vote on the main motion to accept the report. When this report has been adopted, the president should immediately call on the program committee for a report. The program committee chair submits the printed program and moves (or someone else moves) its adoption. This is open to debate and amendment. After adoption by majority vote, it can only be changed by a two-thirds vote of those voting, or by a majority vote of the enrolled membership.

When the membership of the convention and the program has been decided, the convention is ready for business as set forth in the program. The two committees, though they have made their reports, are continued through the session. Supplementary reports may be required from them. Additional delegates may arrive. Speakers on the program may be be absent or ill, or changes in the program may be necessary for other reasons. These two committees should be allowed at any time to make additional reports. This business is conducted as described in the preceding section, but, of course, the program must be followed. Boards, standing committees, and the treasurer are always required to submit annual reports. Reports are sometimes required from other officers.

Officers and the board of managers, etc., are generally elected annually. Some constitutions make the term of office two years. Some additionally provide that only about half the officers should be elected at any one annual meeting. In most organizations it is better to have the term of office begin at the close of the convention, so that the same officers will serve throughout the meetings.

The minutes of the preceding day are read and approved each day at the beginning of the first meeting. If there is no time to read the minutes of the last day at the close of the convention, a motion should be adopted authorizing the board, or some committee, to approve the minutes of that day. When the proceedings of a convention are to be published, as they usually are, a publishing committee should be appointed and should have the power to edit the proceedings. When its business is done the convention adjourns *sine die.*

(71b) A Convention not yet Organized. Like a mass meeting [69] a convention ***not yet organized*** has no constitution, by-laws, or officers when called to order. It has the added difficulty of determining who is entitled to vote. In a mass meeting everyone may vote, but in a convention only the properly appointed delegates may vote. This is sometimes a question difficult to determine with fairness. A committee or group calls the convention and makes all preliminary arrangements for the meeting. If the convention is large, requiring the reservation of a hall for the delegates, the committee should allow only those to enter who have *prima facie* evidence of their right to membership. In contested cases both sides should be admitted. The chair of the organizing committee should call the convention to order. Either the chair or someone the committee has selected for the purpose should nominate a temporary chair and a temporary secretary. Next should come the appointment of a committee on credentials, whose duty it is to examine all credentials and report a list of all the delegates who are entitled to seats in the convention. When alternates have been appointed, they should be reported also. While the committee on credentials is out, committees may be appointed on nominations of officers, on rules, and on order of business or program. In a large convention of this kind, all committees should be appointed by the chair, and no one whose right to a seat is questioned should be placed on a committee until the convention has acted favorably on his or her case.

Until the committee on credentials has reported, the only business that can be done is to authorize the chair to appoint the above-mentioned committees. While waiting for the committee on credentials to report, time is usually spent in listening to speeches. When the committee reports, the procedure is the same as for an organized convention. After the report is adopted, the convention proceeds to its permanent organization, acting on the reports of the other three committees previously appointed, taking them in whatever order suits the convention. When these reports have been acted upon, the convention is organized—with members, officers, rules, and a program—and its business is transacted as in other organized deliberative assemblies. If the convention adopts rules only for the session, the committee on rules need recommend only a few rules as to the hours for beginning the meetings, the length of the speeches, etc., and a rule adopting some standard rules of order, where not in conflict with its other rules. If it is not intended to make a permanent organization, the organization just described is all that is necessary.

If the convention is called to form a permanent organization, the committee on nominations is not appointed until after the by-laws are adopted, and the committee on rules should report a constitution and by-laws as in the case of a permanent society **[70]**. In such cases, the committee is more often called the committee on constitution and by-laws. When a convention of this kind is composed of delegates away from their homes, it is practically impossible to have them assemble more frequently than once a year. Therefore, the persons interested in calling the convention should carefully draft a constitution and by-laws before the convention meets. Those who draw up the by-laws should be appointed on the ***committee on constitution and by-laws*** in order to avoid delay in reporting them.

After the committee has reported a constitution and by-laws the procedure is the same as described in **70**.

When the by-laws are adopted, the officers are elected and committees are appointed as prescribed in the by-laws. The convention is then ready to go to work.

Article XIII: Legal Rights of Assemblies and Trial of Their Members

72. Right of a Deliberative Assembly to Punish its Members. A deliberative assembly has the right to make and enforce its own laws and to punish any member who violates them. The extreme penalty is expulsion of a member from the society. If the assembly is a permanent society, it has the right for its own protection to give public notice of a member's expulsion from the society and the termination of his or her membership in it. An assembly, however, has no right to go beyond what is necessary for self-protection and to publish the charges against the member. In a case where a member of a society was expelled, and an officer of the society published, by its order, a statement of the grave charges upon which he had been found guilty, the expelled member recovered damages from the officer in a suit for libel, the court holding that the truth of the charges did not affect the case.

73. Right of an Assembly to Eject anyone from its Place of Meeting. Every deliberative assembly has the right to decide who may be present during its sessions. When an assembly, either by a rule or by a vote, decides that a certain person should not remain in the room, it is the duty of the chair to enforce the rule or order, using any force necessary to eject the person.

The chair can detail members to remove the person without calling upon the police. Anyone who uses unnecessary force to remove the person is liable for damages, just as a policeman would be in a similar situation. Whatever abuse the person may suffer when being removed from the room, neither the chair nor the society is liable for damages, because, in ordering the person's removal, they do not exceed their legal rights.

74. Rights of Ecclesiastical Tribunals. Many deliberative assemblies are ecclesiastical bodies. It is important to know the extent to which civil courts respect their decisions. The Supreme Court has laid down the broad principle that when a local church is but a part of a large and more general organization or denomination, the court will accept as final the decision of the highest ecclesiastical tribunal to which the case has been carried within that general church organization on all questions of discipline, faith, or ecclesiastical rule, custom, or law, and will not inquire into the justice or injustice of its decree as between the parties before it. The officers, ministers, members, or the church body that the highest judiciary the denomination recognizes, the court will recognize. Whom that body expels or cuts off, the court will hold to be no longer members of that church. The court laid down these principles:[1] (a) "Where a church is of a strictly congregational or independent organization, and the property held by it has no trust attached to it, its right to the use of the property must be determined by the ordinary principles which govern ordinary associations." **(b)** "Where the local congregation is itself a member of a much larger and more important religious organization and is under its government and control and is bound by its orders and judgments, its decisions are final and binding on legal tribunals." **(c)** "Courts having no ecclesiastical jurisdiction, cannot revise or question ordinary acts of church discipline; their only judicial power arises from the conflicting claims of the parties to the church property and the use of it."

75. Trial of Members of Societies. Every deliberative assembly has the right to maintain its own standards, and the right to investigate the character of its members. It can demand the testimony of any member, under pain of expulsion if refused. Charges against members are usually referred to a standing committee whose duty it is to investigate and report cases for discipline. Reports don't have to be detailed. They recommend the action the society should take, and usually close with resolutions covering this. When expulsion of a member is recommended, the ordinary resolutions are *(1) to fix the time to which the society shall adjourn;* and *(2) to instruct the clerk to cite the member to appear before the society at this adjourned meeting to show cause why he or she should not be expelled upon the charges* (which should then be indicated). After charges are preferred against a member, and the assembly has ordered that he or she be cited to appear for trial, the member is theoretically under arrest and is deprived of all the rights of membership until his or her case is disposed of. No member without his or her consent should be tried at the same meeting at which the charges are preferred, except when the charges relate to something done at that meeting. The clerk should send the accused member a written notice to appear before the society at the appointed time, and should at the same time furnish the member with a copy of the charges. A failure to obey the summons is generally sufficient cause for summary expulsion.

At the appointed meeting what may be called the trial takes place. Frequently, the only evidence required against the member is the report of the committee. After it has been read and any additional evidence is offered that the committee may see fit to introduce, the accused should be allowed to make an explanation and introduce witnesses if he or she so desires. Either party should be allowed to cross-examine the other's witnesses and introduce rebutting testimony. When the evidence is all in, the accused should retire from the room, and the society deliberate upon the question and finally act by a vote on the question of expulsion or other punishment proposed. No member should be expelled by less than a two-thirds[2] vote, a quorum voting. Unless by general consent, the vote should be taken by ballot. The members of the committee preferring the charges vote just as the other members. In acting upon the case, the vast distinction between the evidence necessary to convict in a civil court and that required to convict in an ordinary society or ecclesiastical body must be kept in mind. ***Moral conviction of the truth of the charge is all that is necessary in an ecclesiastical or other deliberative body to find the accused guilty of the charges***

If the trial is likely to be prolonged, difficult, or of a delicate nature, the member is frequently cited to appear before a committee for trial. The committee reports to the society the result of its proceedings, with resolutions covering the punishment that it recommends the society to adopt. When the committee's report is read, the accused is permitted to make his or her statement of the case, and the committee is allowed to reply. The accused then retires from the room, and the society acts upon the resolutions submitted by the committee. The members of the committee should vote upon the case just as the other members. If she or he wishes it, the accused is usually permitted counsel at his or her trial. The counsel must be a member in good standing. The society can refuse to hear, and can also punish, a counsel guilty of improper conduct during the trial.

Notes

ARTICLE I: [I.1] *"Brother Moderator,"* or *"Brother Chairman,"* implies that the speaker is also a moderator or chairman. Such expressions should not be used.

[I.2] In the U.S. House of Representatives there is no appeal from the decision of the chair as to who is entitled to the floor, nor should there be any appeal in large mass meetings, as the best interests of the assembly require the chair to be given more power in such large bodies.

[I.3] In Congress motions are not required to be seconded.

[I.4] H.R. Rule 1, §5, is as follows: "He shall rise to put a question, but may state it sitting; and shall put questions in this form, to wit: 'As many as are in favor (as the question may be), say Aye;' and after the affirmative voice is expressed, 'As many as are opposed, say No;' if he doubts, or a division is called for, the House shall divide; those in the affirmative of the question shall first rise from their seats, and then those in the negative; if he still doubts, or a count is required by at least one-fifth of a quorum, he shall name one from each side of the question to tell the members in the affirmative and negative; which being reported, he shall rise and state the decision." No appeal is allowed in the U.S. House of Representatives. A more powerful chair is in the best interest of large deliberative bodies.

ARTICLE II: No Notes.

ARTICLE III: [III.1] In Congress this motion was given the highest rank of all motions. However, because it was so often used to filibuster, and because there is so little need for it in an assembly that meets daily over sessions of several months, in the last revision of the *Rules* it was omitted from the list of privileged motions. In ordinary assemblies, having short or infrequent sessions, its usefulness outweighs the harm that may be done by its improper use.

[III.2] "All business before the committees of the House at the end of one session shall be resumed at the commencement of the next session of the same Congress in the same manner as if no adjournment had taken place." H.R. Rule 26. In practice this rule is applied to business before the House as well as to that before committees. But unfinished business does not go over from one Congress to another Congress. When a society meets only once in six months or a year, there is liable to be as great a difference in the personnel of the two consecutive meetings as of two consecutive Congresses; only trouble would result from allowing unfinished business to hold over to the next yearly meeting.

[III.3] Congress has omitted this motion from its latest revision of the list of privileged motions, because it has been abused for purposes of filibuster and is otherwise rarely needed.

[III.4] While Congress retains the call for the orders of the day in its list of privileged motions, it has abandoned the use of orders of the day, having instead a detailed order of business with several calendars. It retains special orders that may be made by a two-thirds vote.

ARTICLE IV: [IV.1] In Congress the former practice was to suspend the rule as to the order of business in order to consider a particular bill, but now it is customary "to suspend the rule and pass" the resolution or bill. H.R. Rule 27 contains the following: "1. No rule shall be suspended except by a vote of two-thirds of the members voting, a quorum being present; nor shall the speaker entertain a motion to suspend the rules except on the first and third Mondays of each month, preference being given on the first Monday to individuals and on the third Monday to committees, and during the last six days of a session. 2. All motions to suspend the rules shall, before being submitted to the House, be seconded by a majority by tellers, if demanded. 3. When a motion to suspend the rules has been seconded, it shall be in order, before the final vote is taken thereon, to debate the proposition to be voted upon for forty minutes, one-half of such time to be given to debate in opposition to such proposition; and the same right of debate shall be allowed whenever the previous question has been ordered on any proposition on which there has been no debate."

[IV.2] In Congress the introduction of a question may be prevented temporarily by a majority vote under H.R. Rule 16, §3, which is as follows: "3. When any motion or proposition is made, the question, Will the House now consider it? shall not be put unless demanded by a member." If the House refuses to consider a bill the vote cannot be reconsidered. But this refusal does not prevent the question's being again introduced during the same session. In assemblies having brief sessions lasting usually only a few hours, or at most not over a week, it is necessary that the assembly have the power by a two-thirds vote to decide that a question shall not be introduced during that session. As the refusal to consider the question prevents its renewal during the session, the vote may be reconsidered.

[IV.3] Section 6 of H.R. Rule 16 is as follows: 6. On the demand of any member, before the question is put, a question shall be divided if it include propositions so distinct in substance that on being taken away a substantive proposition shall remain."

[IV.4] See note I.4.

[IV.5] In Congress a motion "may be withdrawn at any time before a decision of amendment." H.R. Rule 16, §2. The rule given above (c), which is in accordance with the common parliamentary law, is better adapted to ordinary assemblies.

ARTICLE V: [V.1] The common parliamentary law in regard to this motion is thus laid down in Section 33 of *Jefferson's Manual*, the authority in both Houses of Congress: "4. When the House has something else which claims its present attention, but would be willing to reserve in their power to take up a proposition whenever it shall suit them, they order it to lie on their table. It may then be called for at any time." But, because of the enormous number of bills introduced each session and the possibility of considering only a small fraction of them, Congress has been obliged to find some way by which the majority can quickly kill a bill. The high rank and undebatability of this motion enabled it to be used for this purpose by simply allowing its mover the right of recognition in preference to the member reporting the bill, and then not allowing a question to be taken from the table except under a suspension of the rules (unless it is a privileged matter), which requires a two-thirds vote. This complete revolution in the use of the motion to lay on the table renders all the practice of Congress in regard to this motion useless for any ordinary deliberative assembly. It is the extreme of a "gag law," and is only justifiable in an assembly where it is impossible to attend to one-tenth of the bills and resolutions introduced. In Congress, to lay on the table and the previous question require the same vote (a majority). In all ordinary societies where to lay on the table is habitually used to kill questions, it should require the same vote as the previous question, namely, two-thirds.

[V.2] The previous question is the only motion used in the House of Representatives for closing debate. It may be ordered by a majority vote. If there has been no previous debate on the subject, forty minutes of debate, to be equally divided between those opposed to and those in favor of the proposition, is allowed after the previous question has been ordered. The motion is not allowed in the Senate. House Rule 17 is as follows: "1. There shall be a motion for the previous question, which, being ordered by a majority of members voting, if a quorum be present, shall have the effect to cut off all debate and bring the House to a direct vote upon the immediate question or questions on which it has been asked and ordered. The previous question may be asked and ordered upon a single motion, a series of motions allowable under the rules, or an amendment or amendments, or may be made to embrace all authorized motions or amendments and include the bill to its passage or rejection. It shall be in order, pending the motion for, or after the previous question shall have been ordered on its passage, for the Speaker to entertain and submit a motion to commit, with or without instructions, to a standing or select committee. 2. A call of the House shall not be in order after the previous question is ordered, unless it shall appear upon an actual count by the Speaker that a quorum is not present. 3. All incidental questions of order arising after a motion is made for the previous question, and pending such motion, shall be decided, whether an appeal or otherwise, without debate."

[V.3] The Congressional form of putting this question is "The gentleman from . . . demands the previous question. As many as are in favor of ordering the previous question will say Aye; as many as are opposed will say No."

[V.4] Congress has abandoned the former practice of allowing the member reporting a bill from a committee to close the debate with a speech after the previous question has been ordered.

[V.5] In Congress the form of this motion is to postpone to a day certain, unless it is proposed to make the question a special order for a certain hour, when the hour is specified.

[V.6] In Congress a motion cannot be postponed to the next session, but it is customary in ordinary societies.

[V.7] Congress has changed its rule in regard to the motion to commit, so that now it is undebatable, instead of being debatable and opening to debate the merits of the main question. In a body like Congress, where nearly all the business must be attended to in committees, debate on referring a proposition to a committee should not be allowed. Members can appear before the committee and present their views. But in an ordinary deliberative assembly it is better to observe the general principles governing the debatability of motion as laid down in **45**, and allow debate as to the propriety of referring the question to a committee.

[V.8] In H.R. Rule 27 is the following: "4. Any member may present to the clerk a motion in writing to discharge a committee from further consideration of any public bill or joint resolution which may have been referred to such committee fifteen days prior thereto. All such motions shall be entered in the journal and printed on a calendar to be known as a 'Calendar of Motions to Discharge Committees.' . . . When such motions shall be called up . . . debate on such motion shall be limited to twenty minutes, one-half thereof in favor of the proposition and one-half in opposition thereto. Such motions shall have precedence over motions to suspend the rules and shall require for adoption an affirmative vote of a majority of the membership of the House."

[V.9] A substitute may be reported by a committee while amendments of the first and second degree are pending as shown in **54 (4e)**. In Congress it has been found best to allow a substitute and an agreement thereto while two amendments are pending. The House rule as to amendments is as follows: "When a motion or proposition is under consideration a motion to amend and a motion to amend that amendment shall be in order, and it shall also be in order to offer a further amendment by way of substitute, to which one amendment may be offered, but which shall not be voted on until the original matter is perfected; but either may be withdrawn before amendment or decision is had thereon. Amendments to the title of a bill or resolution shall not be in order until after its passage, and shall be decided without debate." H.R. Rule 19.

[V.10] "No motion or proposition on a subject different from that under consideration shall be admitted under color of amendment." H.R. Rule 16, §7.

[V.11] "A motion to strike out and insert is indivisible, but a motion to strike out being lost shall neither preclude amendment nor motion to strike out and insert; . . ." H.R. Rule 16, §7.

[V.12] While Congress has no rule on filling blanks except the common parliamentary law as laid down in *Jefferson's Manual*, it rarely makes use of this law, but avails itself of its rule that allows of four amendments pending at the same time, namely, amendments of the first and second degree, and a substitute and amendment to it.

ARTICLE VI: [VI.1] See footnote **V.1** for the Congressional practice. As stated there, Congress has abandoned the ordinary parliamentary use of the motion to lay on the table and has converted it into a motion to enable the majority to kill a measure instantly. The Congressional practice in regard to laying on, or taking from, the table is therefore of no authority in assemblies using these motions in the common parliamentary law sense.

[VI.2] H.R. Rule 18, §1, is as follows: "1. When a motion has been made and carried, or lost, it shall be in order for any member of the majority, on the same or succeeding day, to move for the reconsideration thereof, and such motion shall take precedence of all other questions except the consideration of a conference report or a motion to adjourn, and shall not be withdrawn after the said succeeding day without the consent of the House, and thereafter any member may call it up for consideration: Provided, That such motion, if made during the last six days of a session, shall be disposed of when made." This rule is constructed to mean that the motion to reconsider may be made by any member who voted on the question, except when the yeas and nays were ordered to be recorded in the journal, which is done, however, with every important vote.

[VI.3] In Congress it is usual for the member in charge of an important bill as soon as it is passed to move its reconsideration, and at the same time to move that the reconsideration be laid on the table. If the latter motion is adopted the reconsideration is dead and the bill is in the same condition as if the reconsideration had been voted on and lost. These Rules, like the common parliamentary law, carry the bill to the table, from which it could be taken at any time. [See note, **VI.1.**] Unless there is a special rule allowing it, the two motions could not be made at the same time in an ordinary society.

[VI.4] In Congress the effect always terminates with the session, and it cannot be called up by anyone but the mover, until the expiration of the time during which it will be in order to move a reconsideration.

[VI.5] In Congress, where the quorum is a majority of the members elected, and the members are paid for their services, there is no need for this form of the motion. On the contrary, it has been found necessary to provide means by which the majority may, when it pleases, prevent the making of the motion to reconsider by anyone except the member in charge of the measure.

[VI.6] In the early history of the U.S. Congress a call of the house required a day's notice. In the English Parliament it is usual to order that the call shall be made on a certain day in the future, usually not over ten days afterward, though it has been as long as six weeks afterward. The object of this is to give notice so that all the members may be present on that day, when important business is to come before the House. In Congress a call of the house is only used now when no quorum is present. As soon as a quorum appears it is usual to dispense with further proceedings in the call. This is in order at any stage of the proceedings. In Congress it is customary afterward to remit the fees that have been assessed. In some of our legislative bodies proceedings in the call can only be dispensed with when a majority of the members elect vote in favor of so doing.

[VI.7] The term *sergeant-at-arms* should be replaced by *chief of police* or the title of whatever officer serves the warrant.

[VI.8] It is usual in Congress to excuse those who have *paired off*, that is, two members on opposite sides of the pending question who have agreed that while one is absent the other will not vote on the question. *Pairing off* should not be allowed on questions requiring a two-thirds vote.

ARTICLE VII: [VII.1] The time limit should vary to suit the circumstances. A limit of two speeches of ten minutes each is usually suitable in ordinary assemblies. This can be increased or diminished when desirable by a two-thirds vote **[30]**. In the U.S. House of Representatives a member can speak only once to the same question and no longer than one hour. In the Senate there is no limit to the length of a speech. No senator can speak more than twice on the same day to the same question without leave of the Senate, which question is undebatable.

[VII.2] Formerly the member who reported a proposition from a committee was permitted to close the debate in the

House after the previous question was ordered, provided he had not used all of his hour previously.

[VII.3] In the Senate not even two-thirds of the members can force a measure to its passage without allowing debate, the Senate rules not recognizing the above motions. In the House, where each speaker can occupy the floor one hour, any of these motions to cut off debate can be adopted by a mere majority, but practically they are not used until after some debate. H.R. Rule 27, §3 expressly provides that forty minutes, twenty on each side, shall be allowed for debate whenever the previous question is ordered on a proposition on which there has been no debate, or when the rules are suspended. [See note **IV.1.**] In ordinary societies harmony is so essential that a two-thirds vote should be required to force the assembly to a final vote without allowing free debate.

ARTICLE VIII: [VIII.1] Taking a vote by yeas and nays records how each member votes. It is peculiar to this country. It consumes a great deal of time and is rarely useful in ordinary societies. It can never be used to hinder business when the above rule is observed. It should not be used at all in a mass meeting or in any other assembly whose members are not responsible to a constituency. By the Constitution, one fifth of the members present can, in either house of Congress, order a vote to be taken by yeas and nays. In representative bodies this method of voting is very useful, especially where the proceedings are published. The people thus can know how their representatives voted on important measures. If there is no legal or constitutional provision for the yeas and nays being ordered by a minority in a representative body, they should adopt a rule allowing the yeas and nays to be ordered by a one-fifth vote as in Congress, or even by a much smaller number. In some small bodies a single member can demand that a vote on a resolution be taken by yeas and nays.

[VIII.2] The U.S. Constitution requires a two-thirds vote of both Houses to pass a resolution proposing an amendment to the Constitution, to pass a vetoed bill, or to remove political disabilities; a two-thirds vote of either House to expel a member; and a vote of two-thirds of the Senators present to ratify a treaty or convict on an impeachment. The House requires a two-thirds vote to suspend the rules, but is obliged to allow a majority to order the previous question or to limit debate, as otherwise its business could never be transacted. Still, a bill cannot be passed without at least forty minutes of debate, as that is allowed after the suspension of the rules or the previous question has been ordered. [See note **VII.3.**]

ARTICLE IX: [IX.1] In Congress nothing can be "the report of the committee but what has been agreed to in committee actually assembled," so that a report signed by a majority of a committee acting separately was ruled out. In some societies, however, it is often impracticable to have regular committee meetings with a majority present.

ARTICLE X: [X.1] "Though the Speaker (Chairman) may of right speak to matters of order and be first heard, he is restrained from speaking on any other subject except where the House have occasion for facts within his knowledge; then he may, with their leave, state the matter of fact." [*Jefferson's Manual*, §XVII]. "It is a general rule in all deliberative assemblies, that the presiding officer shall not participate in the debate, or other proceedings, in any other capacity than as such officer. He is only allowed, therefore, to state matters of fact within his knowledge; to inform the assembly on points of order or the course of proceeding, when called upon for that purpose, or when he finds it necessary to do so; and on appeals from his decision on questions of order, to address the assembly in debate." [*Cushing's Manual*, §202].

[X.2] In many organizations it is preferable for the secretary to keep his or her original pencil notes in a pocket memorandum book that he or she carries to every meeting. These original notes, as corrected, are approved and then copied into the permanent records. This plan usually results in neater records, but the original notes should be kept until they are carefully compared with the permanent records. In such case it is better to have the minutes signed by both president and secretary as a guarantee against errors in copying.

ARTICLE XI: No Notes.

ARTICLE XII: No Notes.

ARTICLE XIII: [XIII.1] *Watson vs. Jones*, 13 Wallace U.S. Supreme Court Reports, p. 679. This case was decided April 15, 1872.

[XIII.2] The U.S. Constitution [Art. I, §5] provides that each House of Congress may, "with the concurrence of two-thirds, expel a member."

Index

The figures refer usually to the page where the treatment of the subject begins. The arrangement of the work can be most easily seen by examining the Table of Contents (pp.v -x); its plan is explained in the Introduction (p. xxi). If it is desired to find the proper motion to use to accomplish a certain object, turn to page 16. On pages xxix–xxxi will be found a large amount of information about all the motions in common use, which should be carefully studied so that when the facts are needed they can be quickly found. On those pages will be found, among other things, the circumstances under which any of the common motions may be made; the motions that are in order while a specified motion is pending; and whether a specified motion may be debated, amended, or reconsidered, and whether it requires a two-thirds vote, etc. In the Index under the title, "Motions, List of," will be found a complete list of motions. To find the details refer to the particular motion in the Index. It is best always to refer to general subjects first, as under them will usually be found all the details. Look under Adjourn, Committee, Debate, Forms, Vote, etc., for illustrations.